The Textiles of
GUATEMALA

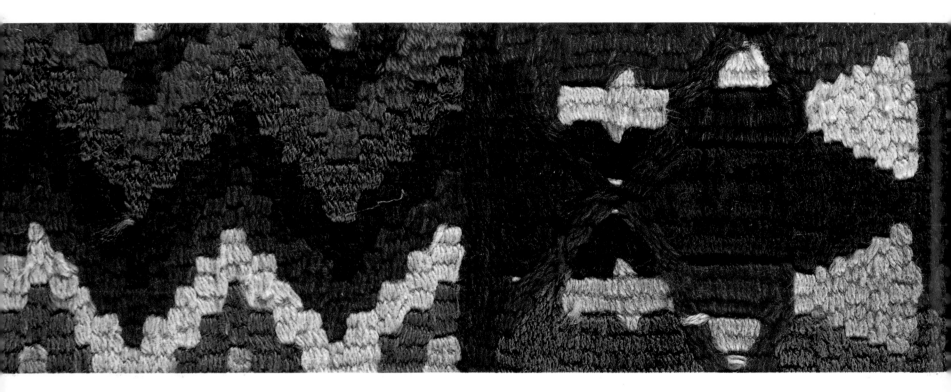

First published in Great Britain in 1991 by
Studio Editions Limited
Princess House, 50 Eastcastle Street
London W1N 7AP

Copyright © 1991 Studio Editions Ltd

Reprinted 1992

The rights of the Régis Bertrand and Danielle Magne
to be identified as the authors of this work
have been asserted by them in accordance with
the Copyright, Designs and Patents Act, 1988.

ISBN 1 85170 812 X

Printed and bound in Spain.

(above)
Woman's belt, Zunil, Quezaltenango
district; Quiché tribe. A couple of figures
standing with arms raised, representing
the *bacabs*, the Mayan gods responsible
for holding up the sky.

(contents page)
Huipil, San Antonio Aguas Calientes,
Sacatepequez district; Cakchiquel tribe,
Symbolic representation of the god of
lightning, 'Kak'.

(page 6)
Detail of huipil, Chichicastenango,
Quicheé district; Quiché tribe.

THE TEXTILES OF
GUATEMALA

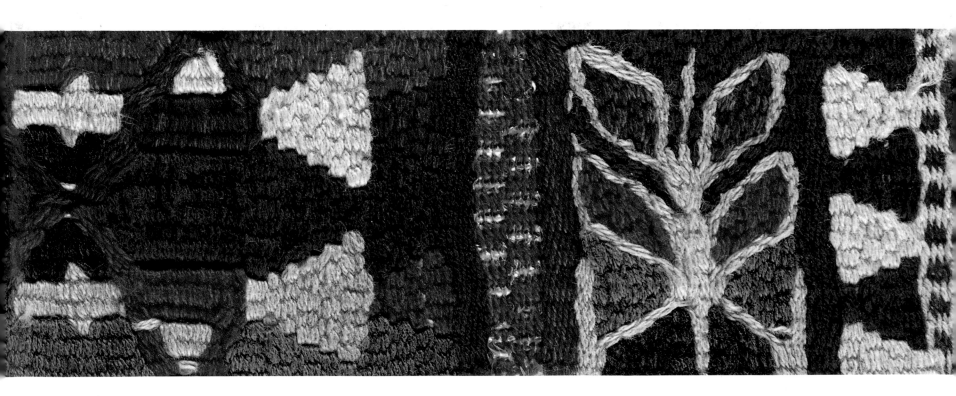

REGIS BERTRAND AND DANIELLE MAGNE

STUDIO EDITIONS
LONDON

PUBLISHED IN ASSOCIATION WITH

LIBERTY
REGENT STREET

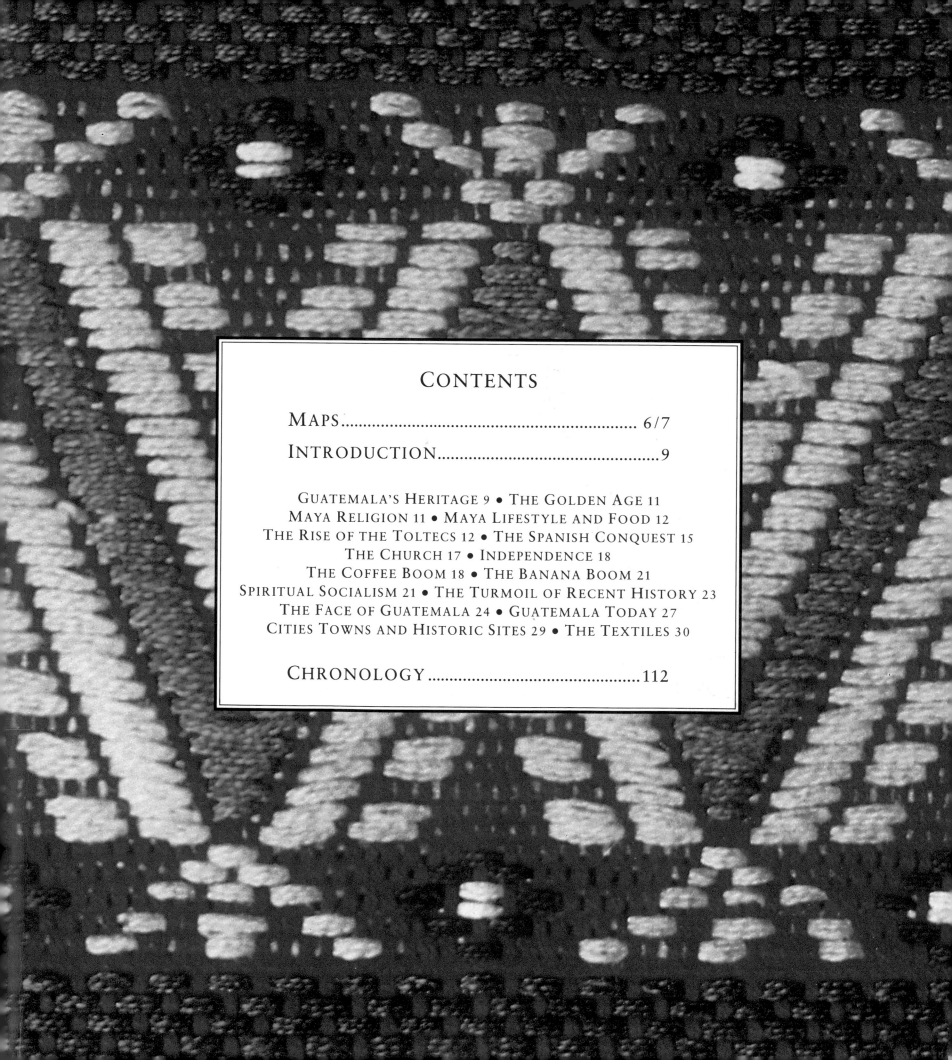

CONTENTS

PETEN

HUEHUETENANGO

ALTA VERAPAZ

IZABAL

QUICHE

SAN MARCOS

TOTONICAPAN

BAJA VERAPAZ

ZACAPA

Chichicastenango

QUEZAL-
TENANGO

CHIMAL-
TENANGO

EL PROGRESO

SOLOLA

Chuarrancho

CHIQUIMULA

Santiago Atitlan

San Juan Sacatepequez

San Pedro Sacatepequez

SACATE-
PEQUEZ

Guatemala City

JALAPA

RETALHULEU

SUCHITEPEQUEZ

Santa Maria
de Jesus

GUATEMALA

JUTIAPA

ESCUINTLA

SANTA ROSA

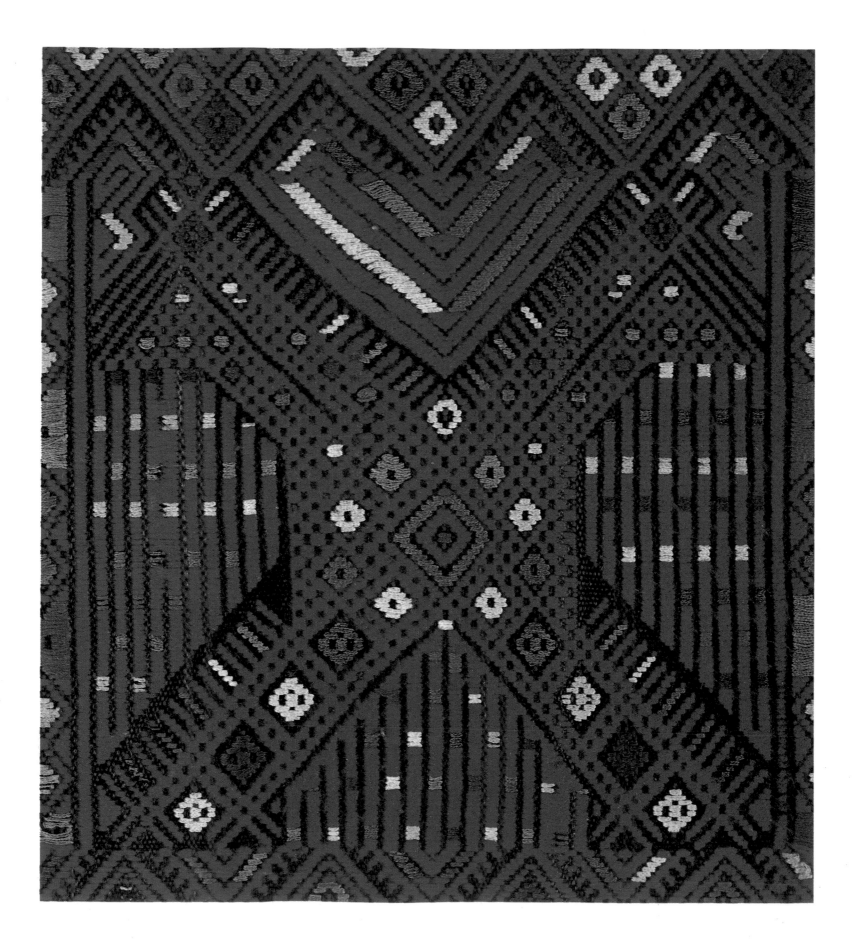

INTRODUCTION

Guatemala has a great and ancient heritage, the origins of which date from well before recorded history as we know it and are surrounded by legends. According to one such legend, two young girls, Ixtaj and Ixpuch, were sent to the river known as El baño de Tohil to wash clothes and bathe. The real purpose of their mission was to tempt three gods to appear. The idea was that the girls should return home with some proof of their success in this venture. When the three gods, Balam Akap, Majucutaj and Balam Quitze arrived they soon realized why the girls were in the river. They spoke to the girls and offered them three coats as proof of their existence. On one coat Balam Akap drew an eagle, on the second Majucutaj drew horse-flies and wasps, and on the third Balam Quitze drew a tiger, each drawing corresponding to the personal symbol of the god. When the drawings were finished, the gods told the girls to offer the coats to their lords, who were to put them on.

On their return, the girls passed on the instructions. The first two lords put their coats on without incident, but the third was stung by horseflies and wasps. In this way the gods were conveying a message of warning and the legend poignantly shows how in folk memory clothes were regarded as somehow symbolic and mysterious.

GUATEMALA'S HERITAGE

The survival of Guatemala's textile tradition is so closely bound up with the country's history, particularly the part played by Maya civilization and culture, that it is helpful to look at the country and the origins of its people.

It is impossible to say when and how Central America was first inhabited, and even the date and origins of the first known ancestors of the Guatemalan Indians – the Mayas – are disputed. Although nomadic hunters probably began arriving from the north in about 25000 BC and there is evidence of settled communities in Central America from about 7500 BC, the first Maya-speaking groups seem to have settled in Guatemala, in the western part, in about 4500 BC. It was not until some three

Man's belt, Nahualá, Sololá district; Quiché tribe. A two-headed bird which is found on ceremonial huipiles of Nahualá, Acatenango and Chichicastenango, inspired by ancient Maya symbols. Here it is shown together with the two-sided disc which represents good and evil. The bird may also derive, though, from the two-headed eagle of Charles v, imposed on the Quiché Indians in the sixteenth century as an emblem of Spain.

Huipil, Chajul, Quiché district; Ixil tribe. A humming bird.

thousand years later, in about 1500 BC, that Maya civilization is known to have begun; it was then – in what is known as the Pre-classic or Formative period – that substantial settlement started, with the building of centres that later became important cities. During this time agriculture was widely practised and there were significant advances in culture and trade. Crafts were developed, especially the making of pottery, calendar systems were devised, and useful contacts were made with the Olmec people of Mexico.

THE GOLDEN AGE

The golden age of Maya culture lasted for about six centuries (AD 300–900) and is known as the Classic period. This was the time when most of the great buildings were constructed and city states developed. It was in this period too that commemorative columns (stelae) were carved with dates, a new type of calendar was introduced, and a recognizable form of writing spread. Carvings in wood and stone show elaborate costumes, at least among the well-to-do, and in the final two hundred years of this period craftsmen painted pottery, carved jade, shell, bone and sometimes marble, and painted temples with bright colours on the inside and outside. All in all, during this stage Maya civilization in Guatemala reached its height, and with the growth in trade and population many Maya centres were larger than European cities of the time.

An important aspect of Maya life during these centuries was the calendar and it was this that made it possible to record precisely the dates of events. Using a method of counting based on multiples of twenty, one of their calendars took the day as a unit in a 260-day almanac, while in another system the so-called 'vague year' was more or less equivalent to our 365-day year. When it came to recording history, the Mayas used a system known as the 'long count', which was based on a period of 5128 years; according to this, we are now in the 'long count' period lasting from 3114 BC to AD 2012.

Alongside interest in numbers and the calendar, the Mayas of the Classic period were much taken up with astronomy and used several sites as carefully aligned observatories. Apart from making surprisingly accurate calculations for the movements of some of the planets, they arrived at impressive figures for the lengths of the solar year and the lunar cycle.

MAYA RELIGION

Linked with the interest in astronomy and calendars, Maya religion was partly based on a particular view of the earth and its place in the universe. It is interesting that colours, which play such an important part in the textile tradition, were regarded as significant in Maya religion and cosmology. Maya religion recognized a collection of gods, though the god Itzamma and his consort Ixchel tended to be seen as the main figures – and again it is notable that such an important goddess as Ixchel was associated with weaving. In their daily life and various needs the Mayas were mindful of the gods and sought to gain their favours by means of elaborate rites, which were preceded by fasting and abstinence and sometimes accompanied by the use of drugs and alcohol.

The remains of temples and paintings, sculptures and pottery testify to the importance of religion in Maya society. The builders of the temples constructed them from limestone, using the almost inexhaustible reserves of this soft and easily workable stone. The scale of these temples was massive: luxury vies with grandiose ambition in the gigantic pyramids dedicated to Chac (god of rain), Ixchel

Huipil, Yepocapa, Chimaltenango district; Cakchiquel tribe. Lozenge design characteristic of the Classic era.

A woman's face, near the Santo Tomas church at Chichicastenango.

(goddess of the moon), Itzamma (god of the sun and of the jaguar) and Yum Kax (the young god of corn).

The love and worship of nature, particularly the sun, which lies at the basis of Maya religion, persists today. Despite the influence of Catholicism, many ancient Maya gods live on, their attributes transferred to Catholic saints. Ancient gods of the rivers, trees and crops are still believed to inhabit the land and are invoked in prayers. Sacrifices and offerings are made to the gods for the well-being of the community, and *rezadores* – Maya prayer makers – often make long and difficult journeys into the mountains in search of the gods whose images still adorn hidden mountain caves. *Brujos* – sorcerors believed to have the power to transform themselves into animals – are sought by villagers wishing to use their powers to cast spells over an adversary; dances for rain and sun to improve the crops are common.

MAYA LIFESTYLE AND FOOD

We also know something of the lifestyle of the Mayas. Society was feudal, with the ruling class, which consisted of priests, merchants and various professionals, living more comfortably in the larger settlements, while peasant farmers lived and worked on the land. The larger settlements, with their nearby smaller rural settlements, were relatively independent, and against this background there developed a mixture of trade and conflict, alliances and warfare.

For food, the Mayas made great use of maize, which formed the basis of their diet, especially among the poorer people. Meat and fish were also eaten, particularly by the ruling classes, and gardens and markets helped in the growing and selling of fruit and herbs. In suitable places there were crops of beans, gourds, chillies and cacao, as well as orchards of fruit trees.

The importance of maize in Maya life is shown by a legend which is central to their beliefs and culture. The *Popol Vuh*, the Book of Time, the most ancient document of pre-Hispanic civilization and the great book of the Ki-tche Mayas, recounts how the ancestral gods Tepek and Gucumatz created the earth from a celestial sea and endowed it with animals and plants. After the creation, avid for praise and veneration, they fashioned creatures in human form from mud. Then a race of beings made from wood appeared, but the gods destroyed these soulless creatures, replacing them with men made of flesh. However, they became evil and were annihilated when black rain fell and a huge deluge swept the earth. Finally, the True Men, the ancestors of the Quichés, were created from corn paste.

This mystical relationship with corn persists to this day. Maize as a crop was first grown by the Mayas during the Classic period; initially, it was sown and harvested only once a year, but as astrological discoveries developed, they were soon able to produce half-yearly crops.

Such was the golden age of the Mayas. From about AD 800, however, there was instability in Central America generally, and within a century Maya civilization went into decline in Guatemala as elsewhere.

THE RISE OF THE TOLTECS

In what was to become a permanently painful way of life for the Indians of Guatemala, political and social unrest quickly turned prosperity into decline. Trade dwindled, wars increased, all new building ground to a halt. By the middle of the ninth century AD many of the cities had been abandoned and fallen into ruin. The reasons for the fall of the Mayas may never be known. According to one theory,

---

Woman's belt, Sololá, Sololá district; Cakchiquel tribe. The pattern represents ears of corn.

A vegetable vendor wearing a pleated skirt characteristic of San Lucas de Sacatepequez. The skirts are sometimes as wide as five metres at the hem and are held up round the waist with a cord.

a revolt by peasants may have arisen because of dissatisfaction with an increasingly exploitative ruling class – a familiar enough theme in the subsequent history of Guatemala.

By the tenth century most of the Maya grandeur had crumbled into ruin. Fortunately, however, not all was lost. Some cities in what is now northern Belize survived the mass rural exodus and remained populated throughout the Post-classic period, which lasted until the Spanish conquest. The Yukatan peninsula suffered least, but was eventually suppressed in AD 987 by the warring Toltecs from Central Mexico, who introduced, among other things, the ritual of human sacrifice, which finally brought down the curtain on the last remains of pure Maya culture.

By the end of the thirteenth century, even the great Yucatan cities of Chichén Itzá and Uxmal had been deserted. The invasion of a small group of Toltec-Mayas brought about another radical change in life away from religion and peace and towards a primarily secular and militaristic order. The Toltecs quickly established many ruling empires, the most powerful being the Quiché in the centre of the country, the Utatlán to the west and the Cakchiquel to the south. The legacy of these tribes survives today in the number of languages which still divide the Guatemalan highlands.

Most of the archeological remains from this period of Toltec domination confirm a general political instability as the old valley settlements were replaced by fortified hilltop villages. While the population of these groups expanded, the highlands quickly became exhausted and were unable to sustain the agricultural burden. The principal tribes began to fight over food and land, and at the height of this unrest the Spanish arrived, quickly turning the bickering to their advantage.

THE SPANISH CONQUEST

While the highland tribes of Guatemala warred amongst themselves the Spanish conquistadores invaded and captured the Aztec capital at Tenochtitlan in 1521 in what is now Mexico. Under the ruthless leadership of Pedro de Alvarado, the Spaniards wreaked havoc in the most savage manner, establishing the reputation of the conquistadores which has come down to us today.

In 1523 Alvarado was ordered into Guatemala to convert the tribes to Christianity. With 120 horsemen, 300 foot soldiers and 200 Mexican Indian warriors Alvarado headed south from Mexico along the Pacific coast into Guatemala. Defeating a small band of Quiché warriors, he headed north into the highlands where he massacred the main body of the Quiché army numbering 30,000, led by Tecún Umán; legend has it that the battle ended when he was killed in hand-to-hand combat with Alvarado. Ultimately sling-shots proved ineffective against horsemen and gunpowder.

In desperation, the Quichés invited the Spaniards to their capital, Utatlán, where they planned to ambush the invaders. Alvarado grew suspicious, and had the entire city burnt to the ground. Having successfully dealt with the Quichés, he made plans to subdue the remaining tribes. The Cakchiqueles were quick to form an alliance with the powerful Spaniards and Alvarado established his headquarters next to the Cakchiquel capital of Iximché in 1523, from where he launched his attacks to overcome on the remaining tribes.

With the occasional help of his brother Gonzalo, Alvarado's disciplined troops swiftly defeated the Tzutujiles, Pipiles, Mames, Zaculeu and Pokomans. But not every battle went according to plan. The Uspantecs and the Ixil

---

Huipil, Nebaj, Quiché district; Ixil tribe. Humming-bird and horse, together with a human figure.

Huipil, Chajul, Quiché district; Ixil tribe. The humming-bird is symbolically associated with male sexual power; its entrails were eaten to restore energy.

Indians both scored victories over Alvarado as he tried to enter the Cuchumantes. In 1526 the Cakchiqueles turned on their Spanish allies and ultimately forced them out of their headquarters at Iximché.

Alvarado moved to a site close to the present-day town of Antigua, where in 1527 he established the city of Santiago de los Caballeros. It took the Indians a decade to build a cathedral, a town hall and a palace for Alvarado. The surrounding land was distributed amongst his faithful followers. The foundations of Christianity took hold of the countryside field by field, and where the sword would not conquer, the word of God did.

Following repeated attempts by Alvarado to subdue the fierce Rabinal and Kekchi Indians by brute force in the Verapaz highlands, the task was eventually completed by Fray Bartolomé de Las Casas. In 1540, following three years of preaching, he managed to convert the tribes to Christianity and Spanish rule without spilling one drop of blood.

Yet peace was to make Alvarado restless, rendering him starved of battle and plunder. His reputation for brutality eventually reached Spain, where he was summoned to face charges of treason. He was not convicted and returned to Guatemala with a wife. She was to die soon after his return and Alvarado set sail to find adventure in Peru. He subsequently returned to Spain for the last time, where he married his first wife's sister and then took her back with him to Guatemala. Soon bored again with his comfortable family life, he set sail for the Spice Islands, but died in 1541 on the way attempting to quash an Indian uprising in Mexico. His death was to mark the beginning of tribal unrest which has lasted to this day in the region.

At Alvarado's death, his wife took control of the capital and had the entire city painted black to mourn her late husband. Then, in the same year, a series of severe storms hit the country, culminating in the eruption of Agua volcano, which buried the city of Santiago under a wave of mud. The survivors built the second Santiago further up the valley. This city was to serve as the seat of the Audiencia de Guatemala, comprising the provinces of Costa Rica, Nicaragua, San Salvador, Honduras, Guatemala and Chiapas. The city remained the centre of political and religious power for two hundred years, growing in population to 80000, before it was destroyed in 1773 by an earthquake.

THE CHURCH

The influence of the Church on Central America should not be underestimated. Guatemala was first host to the Franciscans, who accompanied Alvarado, then the Mercedarians, Dominicans and Jesuits in quick succession. The country's first bishop, Francisco Marroquin, heaped favours on these religious orders in the shape of land, Indians and tax relief, allowing them to establish their fortunes from sugar, wheat and indigo.

Santiago soon boasted eighty churches, and the power of the Church fostered the splendour of the capital, while openly exploiting the indigenous Indians. Religious orders became great patrons of the arts, accumulating fine paintings, sculptures, tapestries and jewelery. And as the Church grew, so did religious persecution, which was at its worst between 1572 and 1580, when the Inquisition had offices in the capital.

The power of the Church continued to grow unabated for almost two hundred years, until it finally spiralled out of control halfway through the eighteenth century. Spanish kings, wary of ecclesiastical corruption and influence, began imposing taxes on the Church and limiting its power in Central America. In 1767, Carlos III banished the

Ritual at the church entrance, Santo Torres, Chichicastenango. A shaman is burning *pom* – a kind of incense – at the sacred fire which is kept burning on the steps of the church in order to keep away evil spirits.

Huipil, Palo Gordo, San Marco district; Mam tribe.

Jesuits from the Spanish colonies.

Christianity and the ravages of colonialization affected the structure of the Indian population most in the highlands. Scattered tribes were relocated into new Spanish-style towns with a church at the centre. Seven hundred new villages were built between 1543 and 1600. The system allowed better control over the people and enabled the Church to concentrate on indoctrinating the Indians with Christianity. It also removed the last traces of the old tribal factions, which had caused the Spaniards so many problems when they arrived.

INDEPENDENCE

Colonial rule spawned dissatisfaction not only among the subjugated tribes of Central America, but also among the growing number of creoles and people of mixed blood known as *mestizos*. The result created two strains of political rebellion, which to a greater or lesser extent remain to this day in the region: conservatives who side with the church and liberals who want a secular state.

Dissatisfaction developed into the power to overcome oppression the day Napoleon invaded Spain and King Fernando VII abdicated. A liberal constitution was imposed on Spain by France and the repercussions of reform quickly spread through the colonies. Brigadier Don Gabino Gainza, who governed Central America at the time, was forced to sign a formal Act of Independence in 1821, while secretly hoping to maintain the political status quo with the backing of wealthy landlords and the Church. The newly elected emperor of Mexico sent troops to annexe Guatemala, but this union only lasted one year.

In 1823 a second declaration of independence formed a federation of Central American states which abolished slavery and backed liberal social reforms along similar lines to those of the United States Constitution. Under the presidency of General Manuel José Acre of Salvador, the federation members struggled for power in this new order, which was doomed to failure. Liberals from Salvador, Honduras and Guatemala rallied under the leadership of a Honduran general, Francisco Morazon. Religious orders were summarily abolished in Guatemala, as was the death penalty. Trial by jury, a national school system, civil marriage and the Livingston law code came about.

Liberal rule lasted no longer than the Mexican empire. Rebellion from the mountains, under the youthful and illiterate leader Rafael Carrera, soon brought down the government in Guatemala City. Liberal reforms were abolished and the authority of the Church reinstated. The conservatives, realizing Carrera was their only chance of a return to power, sided with this unlikely ally. There quickly followed a war with the federation which culminated in Guatemala becoming an independent republic in 1847.

THE COFFEE BOOM

Despite the many domestic squabbles and foreign invasions, Guatemala managed to develop some economic security through agricultural reform. In June 1871, the liberal revolution, led by Rufino Barrios from Mexico, stormed the country's capital, and quickly won public support and a general election. Once more the Church was overthrown and secularism promoted in its place. For all his militaristic bravado, Barrios was a man who understood the value of commerce. When he gained power in 1871, coffee accounted for fifty per cent of the country's exports. By 1884 the volume of coffee output had increased five-fold.

Barrios also founded the Ministry of Development to promote agricultural trade, extended the railroad net-

---

Joyabaj stall-holder at a market. This Quiché centre has retained many of the festivities established during the colonial period – the *bailes*, or flying stick dance, for instance. The 'stick' is a pole up which the dancer climbs, and then descends, suspended by one foot, whirling dangerously.

Huipil, Santa Catarina Palopo, Sololá district; Cakchiquel tribe. Men and women figure on textiles as *muñecas*, or little dolls, the origin of which is unknown. Women appear more frequently than men, generally with their arms swinging at their sides.

work, established a national bank, and expanded the ports of Iztapa, Champerico and San José to handle new business. By the turn of the century, foreign trade had increased twenty times.

The rewards of trade had a fundamental impact on the social structure of Guatemalan life. The coffee boom prompted an influx of German immigrants who developed many of the biggest plantations. Although World War II forced many of them to leave, the German infuence, both politically and economically, is even now very much in evidence in the highlands, where a small group of wealthy landowners still exists.

As has been the case throughout the turbulent history of Guatemala, the local Indian tribes suffered most through foreign intervention. The coffee boom not only robbed the workers of their freedom, it also stripped them of much of their land. From 1873 the government actively began a policy of land confiscation to expand coffee production. Many uprisings followed into the early part of the twentieth century, but each was put down brutally, and the Indians were forced to seek refuge on higher, less fertile ground. The effects have left them ever wary of foreigners.

THE BANANA BOOM

When Barrios died in 1885, while fighting to unify Central America, Guatemala had achieved a certain degree of political and economic security, albeit at the expense of the native Indians. He was succeeded by a host of imitators who slowly but surely undid most of his pioneering work.

The slow-down in the coffee trade made way for the emergence of the United Fruit Company, from Costa Rica, which was to manipulate Central American power for fifty years with the profits from the banana trade. By 1934 the company owned vast tracts of land around the ex-

panding railway system, exporting over 3.5 million bunches of bananas a year. By 1941 an estimated 25000 Guatemalans were employed by the company. Under the control of Jorge Ubico ninety per cent of all Guatemalan exports now went to the United States. It was the growing relationship with the United States that eventually forced Ubico to expel most of the German plantation owners.

Ubico also embarked upon a progressive programme of social reform, which endeared him to the wealthy landlords and alienated the Indians even further. Despite his success in curbing corruption, his treatment of the local Indians left much to be desired. Under his new vagrancy law, any landless peasant was liable to 150 days work a year on the plantations or else building roads. In 1943 he passed a law allowing landowners to shoot suspected poachers and vandals.

Such despotic power eventually got the better of Ubico, who began to imagine he was the reincarnation of Napoleon. By 1944 social unrest finally took to the streets and Ubico was forced to resign. His immediate successor, Juan Frederico Ponce Viades, was little better and was soon forced into exile.

SPIRITUAL SOCIALISM

The overthrow of Ubico became known as the 1944 revolution. Power was divided between military and civilian factions, and the country soon held a general election under a new constitution. A teacher by the name of Juan José Arevalo won a landslide victory and immediately embarked upon the road to reform, which earned the title 'spiritual socialism'.

Through the expulsion of the Germans, many large plantations fell into the hands of the Arevalo government. Many were turned into cooperatives protected by a new set of laws. The pace of reform slackened in the later years

Vegetable market at Santa Cruz del Quiché.

Farm land on the high plains of Guatemala.

of Arevalo's rule, and elections were scheduled for 1950 to select a successor.

The two candidates were from the military side of the junta. One of them, Colonel Francisco Arana, was assassinated in 1949. Suspicion fell on his opponent Colonel Jacobo Arbenz, but a lack of hard evidence eventually allowed him to continue campaigning. He won the election with sixty-five per cent of the vote and set upon the task of overthrowing feudal society, which angered the American corporations that still drove the Guatemalan economy.

The Law of Agrarian Reform in 1952 sold idle or state-owned land to the peasants for a fraction of its market value. This naturally outraged the wealthy landowners, who watched 884,000 hectares of land transferred to 100,000 landless families. The United Fruit Company lost about half of its farming capacity. Much needed as this reform was, the Indians were more confused than grateful for the land and still felt unable to trust the actions of those in power. The long-term effects were less than impressive, however good the intentions.

Despite the many problems which faced Arbenz, his programme of social reform gathered pace and became increasingly more radical. In 1951 the communist party was officially recognized in Guatemala, winning four seats to the legislature at the next elections. Although the Arbenz government was far from communist, it nevertheless remained wholeheartedly anti-American. Following a series of threats on both sides, President Eisenhower, fearing the country now represented the door through which communism would invade Central America, ultimately decided to overthrow the Guatemalan government forcibly in 1953.

Under the guidance of the new director of the CIA, Allen Dulles, who also happened to be a board member of

the United Fruit Company, an army of sorts was gathered in Honduras consisting mainly of exiles and mercenaries. On 27 June Arbenz stepped down; on 3 July the new government under Colonel Carlos Enrique Diaz was flown to Guatemala aboard a US Air Force plane.

THE TURMOIL OF RECENT HISTORY

A series of military-backed governments quickly undid any hope of genuine social reform. In time-honoured tradition, the people hit the hardest by the latest turn of affairs were the long-suffering indigenous Indians. The constitution of 1945 was scrapped in favour of a return to a more hardline right-wing approach to governing the people. Many unionists and agrarian reformers were killed as a result. And all the while the traditional old-style ruling landlords received economic assistance from the US.

Political unrest quickly dragged Guatemala into economic ruin. Violence and social chaos preyed upon the people. Death squads appeared everywhere, killing peasant leaders, unionists and academics. The most feared death squads were the Mano Blanco and the Ojo por Ojo. An endless string of military leaders continued to grab control – Ydigoras, Marcos Yon Sosa, Turcios Lima, Azurdia and Colonel Carlos Arana Osorio – only to be toppled by others who fared no better. All had one thing in common – the backing of the US president. Even the social reformer John F. Kennedy had authorized a Guatemalan coup in 1963.

To this day, the legacy of political fraud and military violence has kept the rewards of a relatively prosperous foreign trade market well out of reach of the indigenous Indians of Guatemala. Murder became a leader's strongest ally in the fight to maintain power. One such leader,

(*left*) The 'Dance of the Conquest' is the most popular manifestation of indigenous folklore. It tells of the struggle of the Quiché king Tecún Umán and the conquistador Pedro de Alvarado, ending in the bloody victory of the latter. The Spanish wear a mask with curly hair and beard, while Tecún Umán and his men have dark brown Indian masks. It is the mask which creates the character; the costume has little importance.
(*above*) Man's belt, San Rafael Petzal, Huehuetenango district; Mam tribe.

Colonel Arana Osorio, is said to have had 15,000 people assassinated for political reasons. He went on record as saying, 'If it is necessary to turn the country into a cemetery in order to pacify it, I will not hesitate to do so'.

As if to add to the country's misery, a terrible earthquake in 1976 claimed 23,000 lives, injuring another 77,000 and leaving one million homeless. In the turmoil that ensued there were many uprisings against the military, sparking off renewed atrocities. In 1977 President Jimmy Carter stopped all military aid to Guatemala on account of the country's horrific human rights record. Sadly the violence did not stop.

Two leading members of the Social Democrat party tipped to win the coming election were murdered along with a hundred of their members. The man who was ultimately to lead the country until 1982, Brigadier General Fernando Lucas García, is believed to have had over 25,000 people killed while he was in power. His successor, General Mejía Víctores – and he gained power by overthrowing General Efraín Ríos Montt, who had conducted a coup of his own to win the leadership – is the worst criminal offender of them all, having destroyed 440 villages at the cost of 100,000 lives.

It was not until 1985 that another free general election was held in Guatemala, the first of its kind for thirty years. The winner, Vinicio Cerezo, a Christian Democrat, was brought to power on a tide of popular enthusiasm.

Acutely aware of the lingering threat of the military, Cerezo nevertheless managed to present a more human face to his people and the world. Political killing dropped significantly, but not altogether. The fate of the 'disappeared', as they are now known throughout the western world, still haunts a country that has not been at peace with itself for over a thousand years.

Chichicastenango women wearing multicoloured *tzutes*.

THE FACE OF GUATEMALA

Guatemala today is a relatively small country, yet it possesses a rich variety of landscapes. Surrounded by other Latin American countries – Mexico, Honduras and El Salvador – and bounded by a sea and an ocean, the Caribbean and the Pacific, it provides a fascinating mixture of lowlands and highlands, tropical and temperate.

Mountains dominate parts of the country, and the mountain chain across the centre forms a natural climatic barrier and creates a series of terraces, each with its distinctive character. Changes in altitude inevitably mean diversity in climate, and the agriculture practised in the highlands is quite different from that in the lowlands. In both cases, vegetation has to be burned and areas of land have to lie fallow over a certain period of time, depending on the position of the fields on the slopes. Several varieties of corn are grown, with a second harvest of marrows, sweet manioc (cassavas) or peppers.

The agricultural system of the highlands appears to be well-adapted to densely populated areas, as long as the land is good. In the Petén region in the north, however, the large marshy depressions called *bajos* fill with water during the summer but are dry during the winter which makes cultivation very difficult.

In the lowland southern regions there is tropical forest, with acajou (cashew) trees that reach a great height, as well as sapodilla trees that were used for their wood by the Mayas and today produce the base for chewing gum. In other parts of the lowlands, bread trees and fruit trees such as avocado grow.

The fauna of the lower lands is abundant and varied. Deer and peccaries are common, as are monkeys, which are easy to hunt and very popular in native cuisine.

The belt of the Pocoman man, Escuintla district. The most beautiful representation of the god of lightning, 'Kak', here, it is not associated with any other motif.

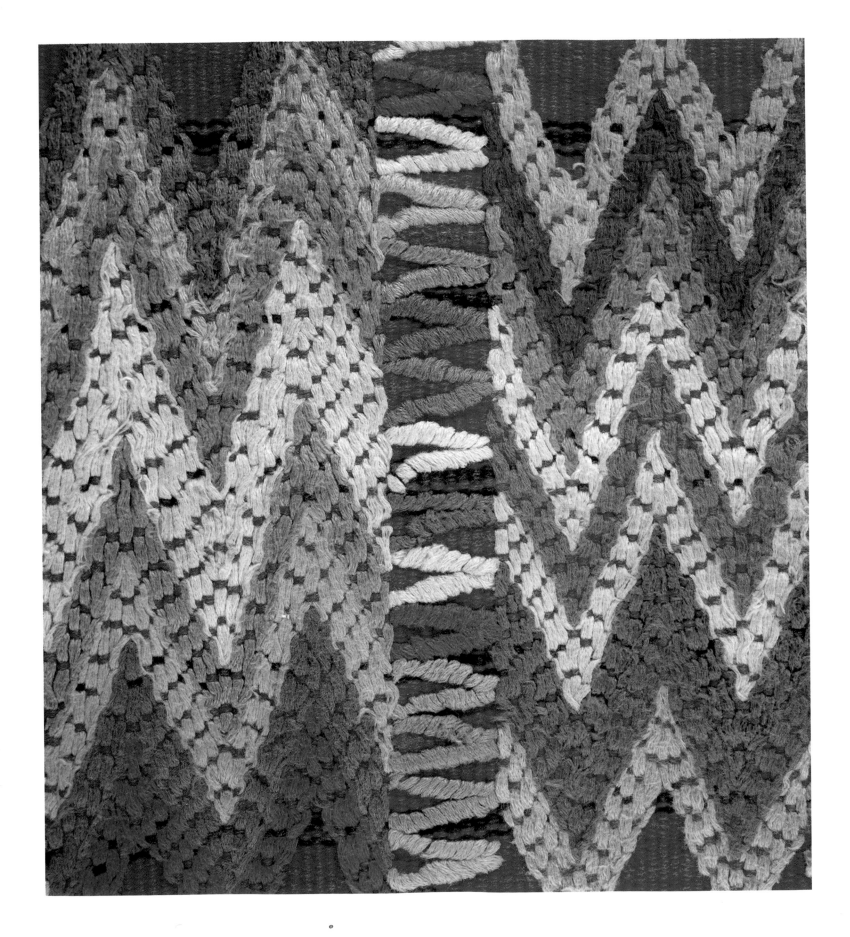

Among the larger birds are turkeys, pheasants and guinea fowl. The most dangerous animals are the jaguar, hunted for its skin, and the tapir, hunted for both its meat and its tough skin, once used to make Mayan armour.

Apart from a certain unpredictability in the climate, Guatemala is subject to natural catastrophe through earthquake or volcano. During the country's history three capital cities have suffered the same fate: in 1541 the first capital of Guatemala, Santiago de los Caballeros de Guatemala, was destroyed by a volcanic eruption; in 1773 the capital, having been moved to a new site, was destroyed by an earthquake; and in 1917 the third and present capital, Ciudad de Guatemala, was destroyed by an earthquake, to be entirely reconstructed at a later date. Then there was the massive earthquake of 1976.

In terms of population and statistics, with 8,200,000 inhabitants Guatemala is the most highly and densely populated state of Central America. Of its 22 regional departments, 8 contain more than seventy-five per cent of the Indian population (Sololá, Totonicapán, San Marcos, Quezaltenango, Huehuetenango, El Quiché, Alta Verapaz, Chimaltenango). Spanish remains the official language of the state, having been the indispensable instrument of colonial domination over the indigenous population. Nevertheless, certain native languages have been maintained: Quiché, Mam, Cakchiquel, Kekchi, Caribe, Xinca, Pokoman, Pokomchi, Chuj, Kanjobal, Ixil. This extreme linguistic diversity accentuates the heterogeneous nature of Guatemala's native people.

GUATEMALA TODAY

Living traditions are very much part of modern Guatemala. Alongside the colourful customs and lore of everyday life,

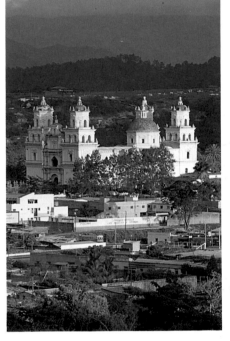

and especially the way of dressing, there are many special events that have roots in the past. Traditional fiestas are held in different places all the time, whether to commemorate the patron saints of cities, towns and villages or to celebrate major events. An outstanding example occurs during Holy Week, when solemn but colourful religious processions are held. Towards the end of the year, on 1 November, All Saints Day is also celebrated; for some reason in Santiago Sacatepéquez huge multicoloured kites are flown on this day.

Looking around Guatemala now, the visitor cannot fail to be impressed by the physical features of the country. There are great mountain ranges, especially the Sierra Madre or Cordillera de los Andes, which runs from east to west, while there are smaller ranges too, including one that forms the boundary with Honduras. A particular feature of the mountains is the presence of volcanoes, which have played an important part in Guatemala's history and even caused the capital to be moved. Volcan Agua provides a suitable vantage point, for from its top it is possible to see most of southern Guatemala and there is a panoramic view of the western highlands, where many of the larger volcanoes are to be found. By way of contrast, Guatemala's rivers and lakes provide another type of scenic beauty and are rich in a diversity of both flora and fauna.

In Guatemala's impressive and ancient heritage, landscape and history are closely bound up with each other, which means that significant archaeological sites tend to be in imposing settings. Obvious places to see are the capital, Guatemala City, the former capital, Antigua Guatemala, Chichicastenango, with its colourful market, and Tikal, with its surviving remains of a Maya city. A dozen other major ancient sites include Ceibal, with its

Huipil, San Pedro Sacatepequez, San Marcos district; Mam tribe. The swan is often associated with the symbol of water in Maya mythology. Here, it is shown together with the ocelot, a small mesoamerican feline, that is symbolically associated with the night and with corn.

The cathedral at Esquipulas.

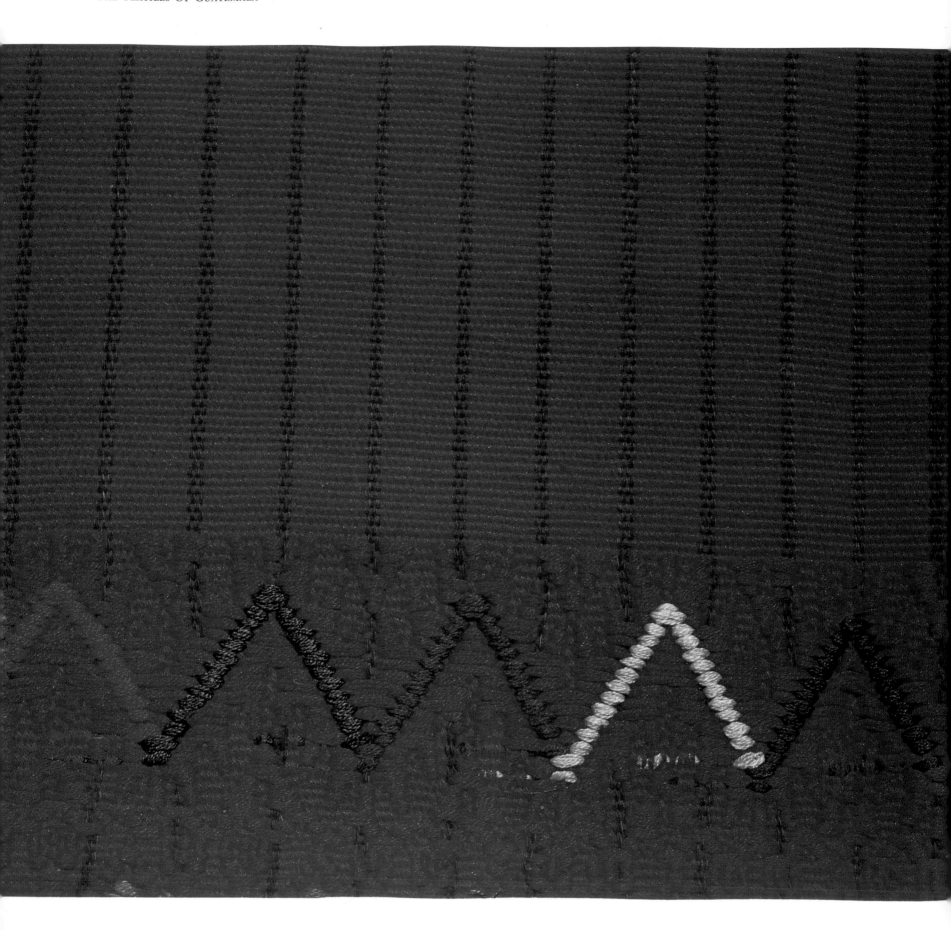

stelae, Yaxha, with its elaborate rectangular pattern of streets, Uaxactum, which had a particularly long life as a Maya city and was the scene of so many important developments in Mayan civilization, and El Mirador, with its massive ceremonial structures. Quiriga contains immense stones with simple Maya carvings, Iximche was an important Maya city that became the first Spanish capital, and Kaminal Juyu has richly stocked Maya tombs beneath its pyramids. Mixco Viejo was a ceremonial centre with two ball courts, Zaculeu contains many temples and a fortress, while La Democracia survives as one of the very oldest of the ancient cities of Guatemala.

CITIES, TOWNS AND HISTORIC SITES

Guatemala has many fine cities and towns, as well as sites of special historic and artistic interest. Ciudad de Guatemala – Guatemala City – which was built as the capital in 1776 after Santiago de los Caballeros, now called Antigua, had been devastated by an earthquake three years earlier, lies on a plateau in the centre of the country. The site has long been known as the Valley of the Hermitage, so named after the hermitage built on a hill in the area. Recent excavations have shown that the present city was built over the ruins of an important pre-Columbian city, Kaminal Juyu. Although the actual size of the former city has never been clearly established, archaeological ruins have been discovered over a wide area and many ancient artefacts have been found.

At this site, the new capital was given a fresh style in architecture. The baroque style, which had prevailed in Antigua for over two centuries, was abandoned, and the neoclassical style was adopted for Guatemala's early churches, public buildings and residences. The traditional

Spanish city layout, with a rectangular pattern of streets and plazas, was retained and dates back to the first years of the rebuilt city.

The earlier capital, Antigua, has left a fascinating heritage and today appears as a place where time has stood still. Many of the city's buildings are as they were in 1773 right after the earthquake. A unique style of architecture evolved during the two centuries of the city's active life in the Panchoy Valley. A baroque form characterized by extraordinary designs in stucco covered with façades of the churches, and today it is possible to see this artistry at the cathedral and a number of churches in Antigua. As a protection against earthquakes, early buildings were given thick walls, low arches, strong pillars and low profiles, and these characteristics have ensured the survival of many buildings to this day in Antigua.

Quezaltenango is the second largest city in Guatemala and it preserves its colonial heritage through its narrow winding streets and the exquisite façade of its cathedral. Since this was the first territory to be occupied by the Spanish conquerors, the region all around Quezaltenango has the oldest colonial buildings in the country.

Totonicapán is a smaller city, but it contains numerous religious and civic buildings with valuable works of art from colonial times. Of special interest is the church of San Andreas Xecul, the façade of which depicts the colour and design of the local *huipiles* or embroidered blouses. Another regional capital, Huehuetenango, has outstanding churches, and the surrounding countryside also has fine examples of colonial architecture. Yet another regional centre is the town of Chimaltenango, which was once considered as the possible national capital. Here there are large churches built by the Franciscan missionaries, and there is a mixture of local

---

(*left*) Huipil, San Antonio Nejapa, Chimaltenango district; Cakchiquel tribe. The colour red is the Maya symbol for the east and the zig-zag symbolizes the snake.
(*above*) Before arriving in Monostenango, 2,250m above sea level, a curious landscape of rocks appears amidst the

pines, the *riscos* of stone and silica, worn by erosion. Momostenango is a large weaving centre where indigenous tradition is still very much alive: the first day of *tzolkin*, the 260-day calendar of the ancient Mayas that still orders the lives of the people, is still celebrated here.

crafts as well as some nearby workshops where special techniques with primitive paints are practised.

Other towns and villages of special interest lie in the area around Lake Atitlán, and in the area of Quiché there are notable examples of colonial architecture in the local capital, Santa Cruz, Chichicastenango and Sacapulas. For colonial art and religious images the lower region is outstanding, while there are many beautiful churches in the upper region of Verapaz. In the eastern part of the country there are more examples of colonial architecture, and other special features there are the Black Christ of Esquipulas, in Chiquimula, and the old pilgrim route that leads there from Honduras. Over on the Caribbean coast, fortresses can be seen surviving from the seventeenth century, when they were built as a defence against pirates.

THE TEXTILES

Guatemala possesses one of the few living craft traditions which have survived centuries of change. It is remarkable that this country, with the unpredictable violence of its tropical climate, the instability of the earth's crust, the explosion of war at the time of the Spanish conquest, and the accumulation of several centuries of natural and cultural aggression, should have retained its identity. Even if aspects of it have sometimes become obscured and lost, its core remains, strong and vibrantly expressed in the craft of its people, where superstition, fetishism and magic mix together with the beliefs born of the interaction between Catholicism and ancient ritual practices.

Under Spanish rule, the Mayas were forced to adopt at least certain aspects of Hispanic dress, partly in an effort to make them integrate with the ruling society, partly to render more acceptable those forms of dress which shocked and were considered immoral by the Catholic Spaniards.

In the warmth of the Guatemalan climate, women were made to cover their breasts with Spanish-style blouses and sometimes even to cover their entire bodies in accordance with accepted missionary style. Thus many aspects of Guatemalan costume which today are considered traditional are not Mayan in origin, but Spanish. This is particularly true of the male costume. The truly traditional male garment was a kind of loincloth, called an *ex*, which is now no longer worn; this is a long band of cloth wrapped around the waist and passing between the legs.

The two ends are sometimes embellished with embroidery and feathers which fall in front and behind. The male garment almost always left the torso naked, apart from heavy necklaces and jade collars loaded with pendants and badges. This costume remained unchanged until the sixteenth century, when Hispanic costume replaced it. The traditional female dress is an ample, white tunic, decorated and similar to the present *huipil*.

From what we know of Maya costume, as depicted in the artefacts which remain today, the head-dress was one of the most important and exotic elements, a composite and multicoloured structure where masks of animals or gods, jade, feathers and braided fabrics sit on a wooden or reed frame, surmounted by immense green and gold plumes. These are the feathers of the *quetzal*, the bird which is the traditional symbol of Guatemala. A turban-like hat seems to have been fashionable too among servants and musicians.

The traditional Maya footwear is familiar from the many pictorial representations which exist. This is the *xanab* sandal, which the Indians still wear nowadays. It is held securely on the foot by two straps which pass between the big toe and the second toe, and the third and fourth toes respectively, and by a knot at the end of the foot. The heel is protected by a finely decorated piece of leather which

Zunil woman wearing an enormous mauve *tzut* standing in front of a wash-tub.

Huipil, Tajumulco, San Marcos district; Mam tribe.

is often long enough to cover the ankle like a short boot.

The dazzling colours and designs of Guatemalan weaving continue to reflect Maya traditions. While many of the designs and their meanings have been lost, many remain, immediately recognizable in the form of geometric patterns and stylized birds and animals reflecting the sense of order and love of nature of the Mayas that is still shared by Guatemalans today. Ancient myths and beliefs become imbued with regional and personal meaning as the weaver incorporates the elements of style particular to her village and creates, inevitably, some elements which reflect her own personality and feelings. Local differences are important and marked: dress performs not just a practical function, but serves to identify the precise origins of a person, sometimes also indicating their social status within the village.

Today, many women have had to give up weaving. Wives whose husbands have died or been killed by the military must take on the man's work; younger people are attracted away from traditional crafts to work in industry; market forces dictate village life. Many women, however, struggle to keep on weaving in their spare time, and if this means that a garment may take several months to complete, it at least ensures the continuation of a tenacious tradition. Weaving remains women's greatest source of pride, and a young girl may offer her first *huipil* to a Catholic saint (echoing the Maya goddess Ixchel) for protection and blessing of her future efforts.

Whilst most of the weaving is done by women, it is the duty of the men to produce articles for sale in the markets. Surprisingly to the outsider, perhaps, it is the men who crochet *morales*, the bags often used to carry tortillas or tamalitos, which are eaten as the midday meal by the Guatemalans when they work.

MATERIALS

The native tribes of Guatemala use a great variety of fibres of both vegetable and animal origins to make their clothes and accessories. Cotton was important from an early stage. King Hunalpu, the second Quiché king, popularized cotton by colonizing the lowlands of the Pacific coast, and bringing Quiché and Cakchiquel Indians from the cold regions of the high plains to produce it. Thus he ensured the production of the essential material for weaving the garments of the inhabitants of the high plains. At this time, the cotton was of different colours – red, yellow, violet, green, orange and *ixcacao* (brown) – while today it is white or occasionally brown.

Although silk as we know it, produced by the silkworm, was not known until the colonial era, before the arrival of the Spaniards certain fibres very similar to silk were used. They come from two different sources – vegetables (*Urtica* or the nettle genus) and insects (spiders, *gusano de guayabo* or guava worm, and *hylesia*). Linen is no longer used by the natives. It was initially propagated during colonial rule, but an interdict from Spain protecting the Spanish monopoly prevented the extraction and weaving of it.

Among the vegetable fibres used, there are different kinds of *maguey*, *corozo*, *izote*, *escobillo*, *hennequin*, *sisal*, *mezcal*, *mezcalito* and *pita flora*. The fibre of *escobillo* (teasel) is much in demand for making *mecate* cords. All of these vegetable fibres have an enormous importance for the natives because they are the basis of the production of accessories. At San Pablo la Laguna, *maguey* weaving is carried out in the following manner: the leaves are hammered with a wooden pestle, then with a little comb the pulp of the fibre is separated and afterwards washed in the waters of Lake Atitlán. After drying them in the sun to whiten them, they separate out each fibre. The natives of

Market at Santiago Atitlán. A woman selling belts from Santiago in front of a superb display of richly decorated trousers and *huipiles*.

Belt, Aguacatan, Huehuetenango district; Aguacateca tribe. Characteristic chevron design.

33

the Acatenango region specialize in using the *pita flora*. The leaves, once washed, are placed in a grinder. The pulp, after being separated from the fibre, is then dried in the sun. Acrylic, manufactured in Guatemala, is very popular and is used in a number of motifs in both cotton and wool weaving.

DYEING

Today the natives who continue the weaving tradition no longer dye their thread themselves. They buy it in the village market, threaded and dyed in the factory. Colours with an aniline base have replaced the animal, vegetable or mineral dyes used traditionally since the pre-Colombian era. They don't resist sunlight and repeated washing as well as the natural dyes; the clothes lose their brilliant colours and fade.

Indigo blue is obtained from clay, anil, *xigiolite* or *sacatinta*, plants which grow exclusively in hot regions. By acidifying the liquid of the *sacatinta* it is also possible to obtain a red dye. Red is normally obtained from the extract of cochineal and *achiote* (also used as a spice), brown from the bark of the *nance* tree and from a type of wood known as *aliso*. The colour green comes from the liquid of the *curcuma* (a root similar to ginger), with the addition of anil and *campeche*. For the yellow, iron hydroxide or sometimes blackberry tree is used; in the region of Alta Verapaz, they use a root named *camotillo*. The violet colour which gives the greatest value to a piece of weaving is extracted from a mollusc, *Purpura patula*, found on the coasts of Costa Rica and Nicaragua. This is the colour used on the *huipiles*, the colour of holidays (*de rezar* – days of prayer) and of people of various religious fraternities.

At Monostenango, the village best known for its woolen weavings, the wool is dyed in a different manner. To soften them, the weavings are soaked in the sulphurous local waters and combed with the *quich*, a kind of warm roller made of dried flowers.

WEAVING METHODS

The most commonly used weaving loom is horizontal, used by the women at home. This is called the *telar de palito* and is made of pieces of dry wood between which are the threads of the warp and the weft are suspended. A strap is tied around the waist of the weaver, while the other end of the loom is attached to a tree branch. The vertical loom, imported from Europe and known as the *telar de pie*, is used by men to produce articles destined for sale in the markets.

The *huipiles*, *tzutes*, napkins and small articles come from the horizontal loom. Belts and ribbons for the hair (*cintas*) are made on smaller looms. Shawls (*perrajes*), skirts (*yergas*), coats and woollen weavings come from the vertical loom, the main manufacturing centres for which are Totonicapán, Quezaltenango and San Marcos. The colours are imprinted on the fabrics with silver stamps, but there are also stamps with a design in negative, so that all kinds of motifs can be printed.

Hand weaving is still widely practised. Almost without exception the women weave, at least for their own needs. A Mayan girl normally owns a loom, which will probably be buried with her. She cannot hope to make a good marriage unless she knows how to weave well.

MALE AND FEMALE COSTUME

The female costume is composed of a number of pieces, including the *huipil*, which is a sumptuously decorated blouse, sleeveless but so wide that it covers part of the arms. The largest *huipiles* (from Chemal and Todos Santos

Selling coloured yarn at the market at Chichicastenango.

Market stall selling pigments, Guatemala City.

Cuchumatanes) fall as far as the knees; in Palín they don't even hide the navel. In San Antonio Aguas Calientes, Quezaltenango or Totonicapán they slip inside the skirt and cling to the body. In Tecpán, the decorations are made on a separate ribbon and then attached to the blouse; in Quezaltenango, they use a special kind of embroidery; in Chichicastenango, they have discs of black silk. If a women is unmarried she has the right to cotton embroideries, whilst the married women wear silk ones; completely white for an adolescent, pretty coloured ones if she has a husband.

The skirt (*enaga*, *refago*, *corte*, *morga*) is rolled up (in Chichicastenango, Zunil, San Pedro Sacatepéquez) or folded, sometimes being as wide as five metres. It is held up by a cord and falls to ankle length. The skirts come in five types of colours: *morga* (dark blue with white stripes San Juan de Sacatepequez), *jaspeado* (with variations of the colours of the Quiché), yellow silk with stripes (the Mam tribe of San Marcos), red in the Ixil region (Nebaj, Chajul), dark in Huehuetenango.

Belts too are found in many different varieties: with symbols of animals along them (Totonicapán), yellow and green (San Pedro Sacatepéquez, San Marco), fuchsia red (San Antonio Alotenango), in wool of different colours with pom-poms on the ends (San José Nacahuil), or finely woven with embroideries in wool representing symbols of *plumas* (a dance from the south of Mexico).

The *tzut* is a woven piece which has a great variety of uses: a scarf around the neck embroidered with mythical animals and ending in a fringe (Nahualá); rolled around the head (Sololá); hanging down the back to pad against objects being carried (Santa María de Jesús). A variation of the *tzut* is the woven napkin which is used for carrying food and tortillas. The *tzut* or *lienzo* can be used to cover

children carried on the shoulders. Scarves four metres long and five centimetres wide make extravagant and original head-dresses. In Santiago Atitlán, the women use a type of band rolled flat like a disc and worn perched on the top of the head, called a *tocoyale*. White or black straw hats decorated with ribbons or with a *sut* protect against the sun.

The shawl or *perraje* is used against the cold or in church. Each end has a large woollen or cotton pompom. Sometimes it is worn in a very particular fashion on the arm or the head, over the head-dress. The *chacale* or necklace is certainly the most important element of clothing for the Indian women. It is made of coral with a heavy silver cross at the end, made of little pieces of silver money separated by a small pearl, between which hang different silver figurines and *juguetillos* (playthings).

Each woman wears her clothes until they are completely worn out. Making the clothes is a family affair. The different parts of the costume are made from bands of fabric, never shaped, and hardly ever sewn.

Today's male costume is made up of pants and a pair of short trousers in white cotton with woollen embroidery of different colours. The ponchito (*rodillera*, *yerga*, *delantal*) is a piece of wool with little black and white squares which is rolled around the waist, like a short skirt. It is used mostly in the villages around Lake Atitlán. The jacket is a short, bolero-style tunic with decorative pockets (Cotzal, Chajul, Nebaj), in white or black wool with bands of cotton in colours which represent different motifs (Sololá), black wool, safari style (Lake Atitlán), richly decorated mainly in red and mauve on the very attractive zigzags (Nahualá). The *capisay* is a coat of thick black or dark-brown wool, characteristic of the Huehuetenango region. Made from

Woman's handkerchief, Chajul, Quiché district; Ixil tribe. Embroidery of little figures holding hands.

San Antonio Aguas Calientes Weaving loom. The loom is made up of two parallel bars, each about 60 cm long; the top bar is attached by two cords to a tree branch, the other is secured around the weaver's waist. As the loom is not fixed to a frame, it is extremely portable.

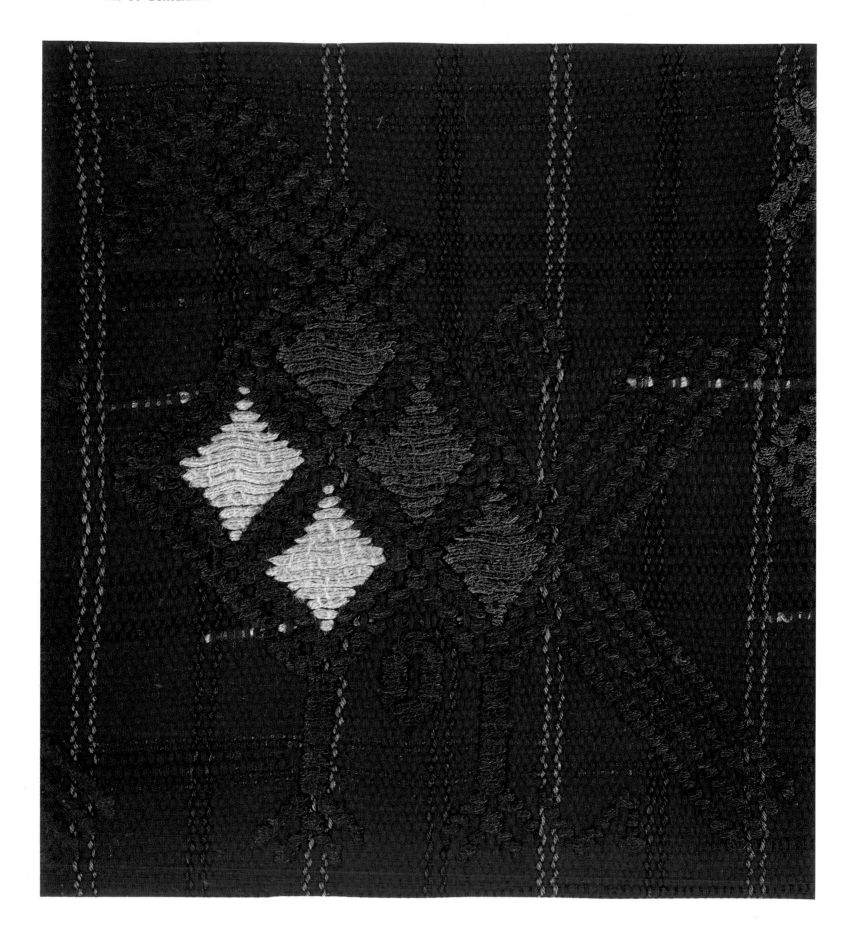

two tails, it looks rather like a priest's chasuble. The sleeves reach up to the neckline like a poncho. The men use the *tzut* like the women, but theirs are produced in different colours and decorated with different designs.

The belt or *banda* varies greatly in its symbols according to the village, but very often the background colour is red. The *mecapal*, a wide belt with tanned leather on the inside, secured on the top of the forehead, serves to support very heavy loads.

The men wear shoes, whilst the women, following pre-Columbian tradition, often still go barefoot. The men wear European-type sandals, simple soles of varying thickness, cut out from old car tyres. The hat, an indispensable element of dress, varies in form, made of plaited straw or wool. Another indispensable element is the bag, called *moral*, *matate*, *bolsa* or *guangochas*. This is a type of haversack made in wool, *pita* (maguey or agave fibre) or cotton according to the regions.

The memory of several centuries of beliefs is anchored and imprinted in these clothes and in the colours of each village. Whether it is the preparation of the thread, the method of dyeing it, the technique used or the combinations of colours, each village has its own methods, its clothes and its symbols. One basic motif can be shared by several villages, but since each community treats it in a different fashion, there will be a great variety of colours and forms. Taking into account the sparseness of Spanish chronicles available, it is difficult to discern the extent of the pre-Columbian influence. Certain motifs, however, such as the snake-bird with two heads, sun-moon, as well as certain animals like monkey-deer, jaguar-eagle, which play an important role in Maya mythology, can reasonably be attributed to this ancient origin.

Geometrical forms, birds, animals, people, plants, flowers, contemporary motifs – this incredible mosaic is the expression of a whole world. Between the Pacific and the Caribbean, between the Tropic of Cancer and the Equator, in this unexpected setting, behind the silence and mystery of its inhabitants, the Maya Empire has left behind an exceptional vision, renewed ceaselessly in these brilliant costumes as they continue to be made today. *Huipiles* and bodices disappear under myriad embroideries of flowers; trousers and belts carry symbols which are impossible to mistake. Despite the paucity of knowledge of this Maya world, the great epic is recounted in each detail of their clothes. The collective creation of a people which history has never ceased to mock and has often threatened with destruction, the traditional costume of Guatemala remains one of the most tangible manifestations of the people's ethnic identity and its desire for expression.

Woman's tzut, Santa María de Jesús, Sacatepequez district; Cakchiquel tribe. Structure of lozenges representing a cockerel.

Huipil, Tactic; Alta Verapaz district.

Huipil, Chichicastenango, Quiché district; Quiché tribe. The word *huipil* comes from Cakchiquel and means 'blouse'. The *huipil* is the decorated part of the woman's costume, embellished with sumptuous and artistic designs. The sleeves are so wide that they cover part of the arms. There are seven types of neckline according to the village of origin; the design is also different depending on whether the woman is married or single.

Woman's tzut, Santa María de Jesús, Sacatepequez; Cakchiquel tribe. Symbolic representation of the cockerel.

Huipil, Tactic, Alta Verapaz district; Pocomchi tribe. Geometric patterns and birds.

Man's belt, San Juan la Laguna, Sololá
district; Tzutujil tribe.

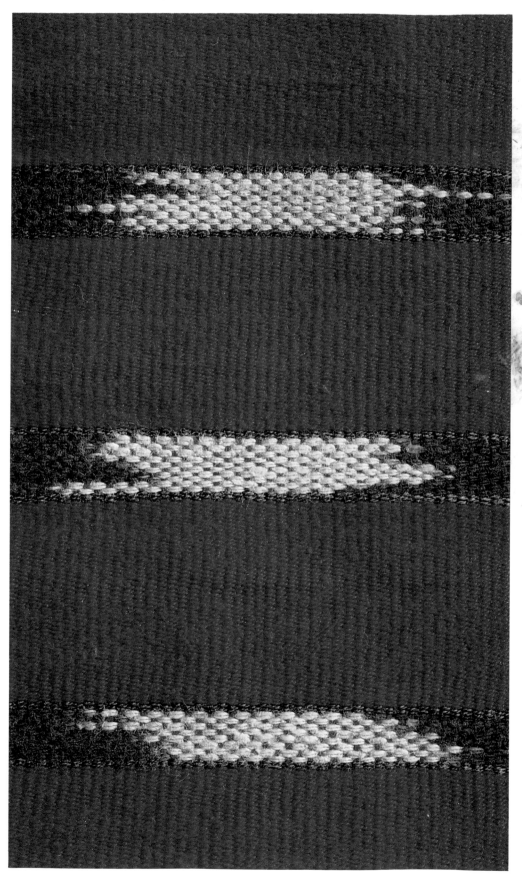

Man's belt, Santa Cruz la Laguna, Sololá district; Cakchiquel tribe.

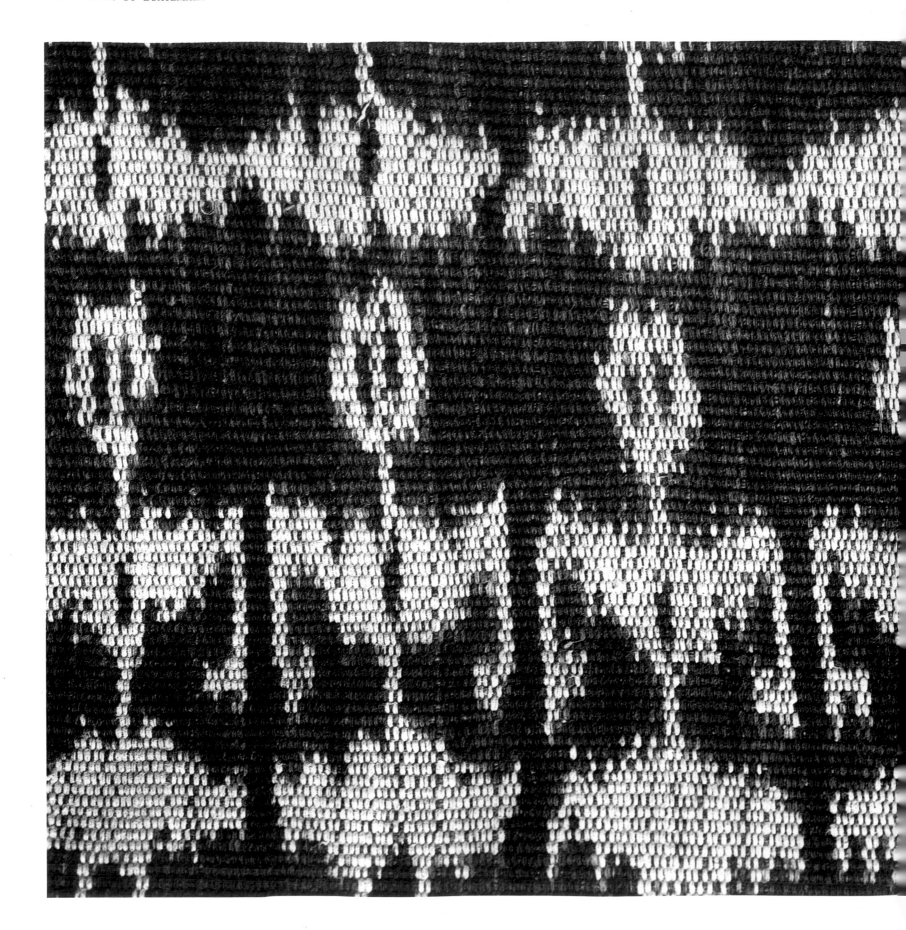

The Pacaya volcano has two craters, one extinct and one active, which spits out smoke and lava. The earth trembles and the heat and plumes of sulphurous smoke create an atmosphere which is almost suffocating. Everywhere lie ponds covered with aquatic plants, even at the summit. The Nobel Prize-winning writer Míguel Angel Asturias describes his country as 'el país de los espejos', or the country of mirrors.

Woman's shawl, Patzun, Chimaltenango district; Cakchiquel tribe. The little figures are obtained by using a technique of dyeing in negative.

The traditional black costume, decorated with symbolic embroideries representing the sun, the rain, the signs of the gods and the stars is always worn by the *principales*, or authorities of Chichicastenango. It consists of a short, fringed jacket, opened over a white cotton shirt, short trousers slit on the thigh and decorated with sun signs; on the head is the *tzut*, made of mauve and red material, with a large tassel in the same colour at each of the four corners, while legs and feet are almost bare in leather sandals similar to those depicted on ancient Maya stelae.

Huipil, San José Nacahuil, Guatemala district; Cakchiquel tribe. Mythological animal from Maya mythology.

Over-huipil, San José Nacahuil, Guatemala district; Cakchiquel tribe. Peacock.

(*right*) Tablecloth representing the *quetzal*, a bird considered sacred in Guatemala since ancient Maya times. The tail feathers are sometimes as long as one metre, and were used to decorate the head-dresses of Maya dignitaries.

Man's belt, Nebaj, Quiché district; Ixil tribe. Geometric forms fitted together, representing the four cardinal points of the earth. This form was popular in the Classic period of Maya civilization and is still widely used.

(*opposite*) Market at Chichicastenango. Thursdays and Sundays are the main market days, the *tangui* of the natives. People come from miles around carrying heavy packages on their backs, in traditional pre-Columbian style, with a leather strap around the forehead called the *mecapal* onto which two cords are tied, supporting the load which sits on the back in one of two large nets called *cascaxte*.

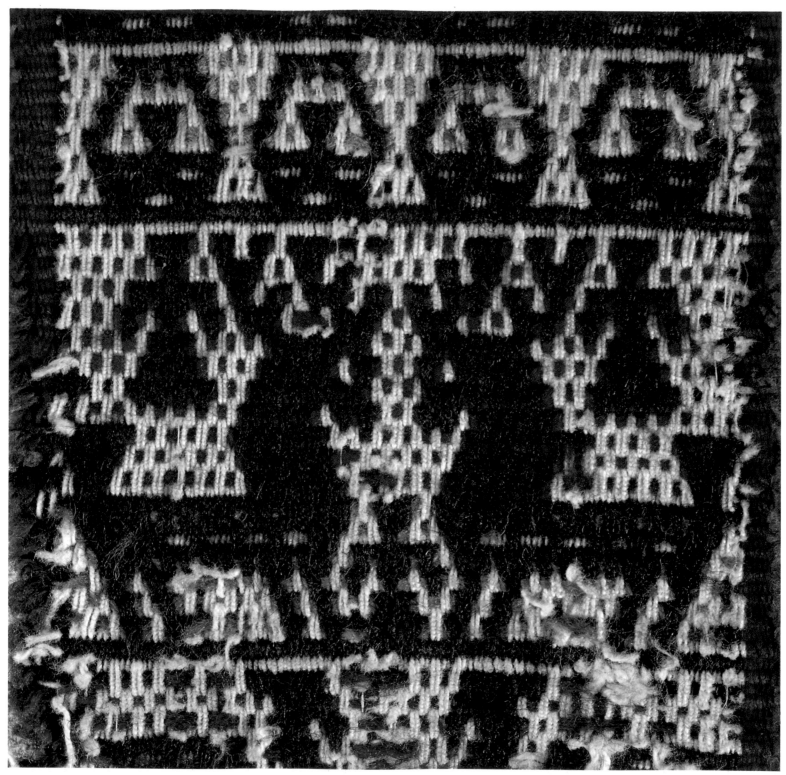

Woman's belt, Totonicapán, Totonicapán district; Quiché
tribe. The deer has a particular significance in Maya
mythology. The dance of the deer, which dates back to
prehistoric times, still holds an important place in
celebrations today.

Woman's belt, Totonicapán, Totonicapán district; Quiché tribe. A scene representing the dance of the jaguar. The jaguar is shown together with the sun in his path through the underworld, where he is the god of one of the nine levels.

Ritual taking place in front of the Santo Tomas church at Chichicastenango. The *principales* kneel on the steps while the shaman burns *pom*, a kind of very strong incense. The Indians are often helped in their prayers by an intercessory shaman who carries their supplications to the Christian God and to the ancestral divinities, the souls of the dead who protect and punish according to the good and bad conduct of the living.

Man's trousers, Todos Santos Cuchumatanes, Huehuetenango district; Mam tribe. The trousers are richly decorated along the leg and are accompanied by a piece of wool called the *maxtate*, which is worn over the trousers around the hips.

Woman's belt, Acatenango, Chimaltenango district;
Cakchiquel tribe.

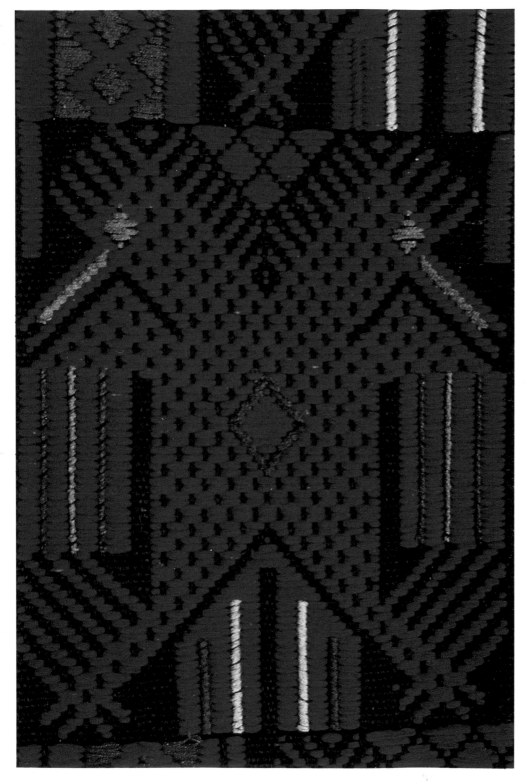

Woman's tzut, Santa María de Jesús, Sacatepequez district. Another representation of the two-headed bird to compare with the one from Nahualá (see p. 8); here, the structure of lozenges is missing, giving it a less cosmic dimension. According to Maya cosmology, when the world was created, man did not play a major role, but was only a supplementary element in the universe, where the planets, the stars and innumerable gods moved in harmonious order. The most important thing for the Mayas was to live without crossing the path of these mysterious and powerful beings who had already destroyed three generations of human beings. All Maya beliefs have a strong dualist element of the eternal struggle between good and evil, with destruction and death dominant factors in their thought. According to the *Popol Vuh*, the sacred bible of the Quiché Mayas, a two-headed eagle is one of the first ancestors of the Quiché Maya race.

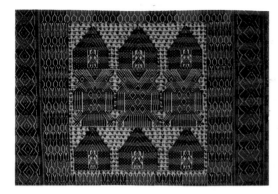

Man's tzut, Palin, Escuintla district;
central Pocomam tribe. Little human
figures appear inside typical Maya
houses, together with two-headed birds.

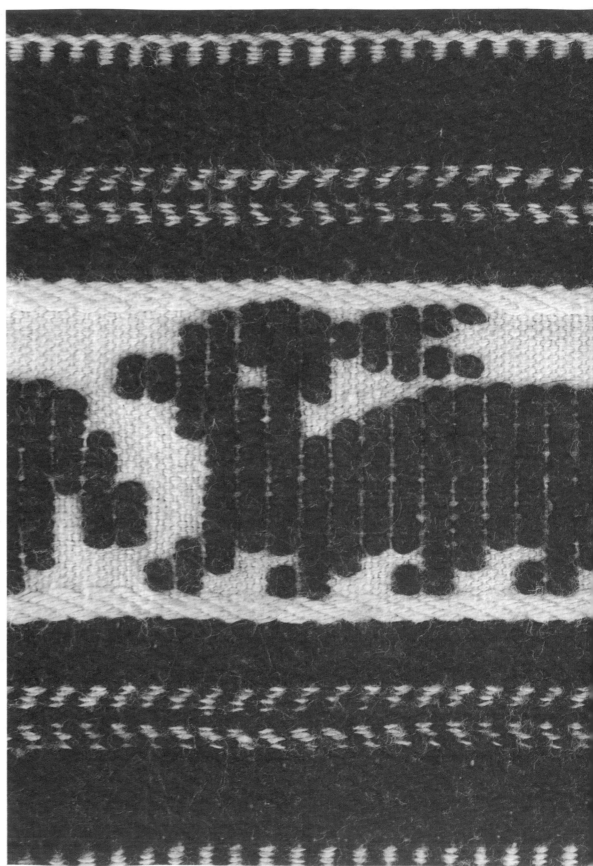

Female tzut, Concepcion Chiquirichapa,
Quezaltenango district; Mam tribe.
Little rabbits walking in Indian file.

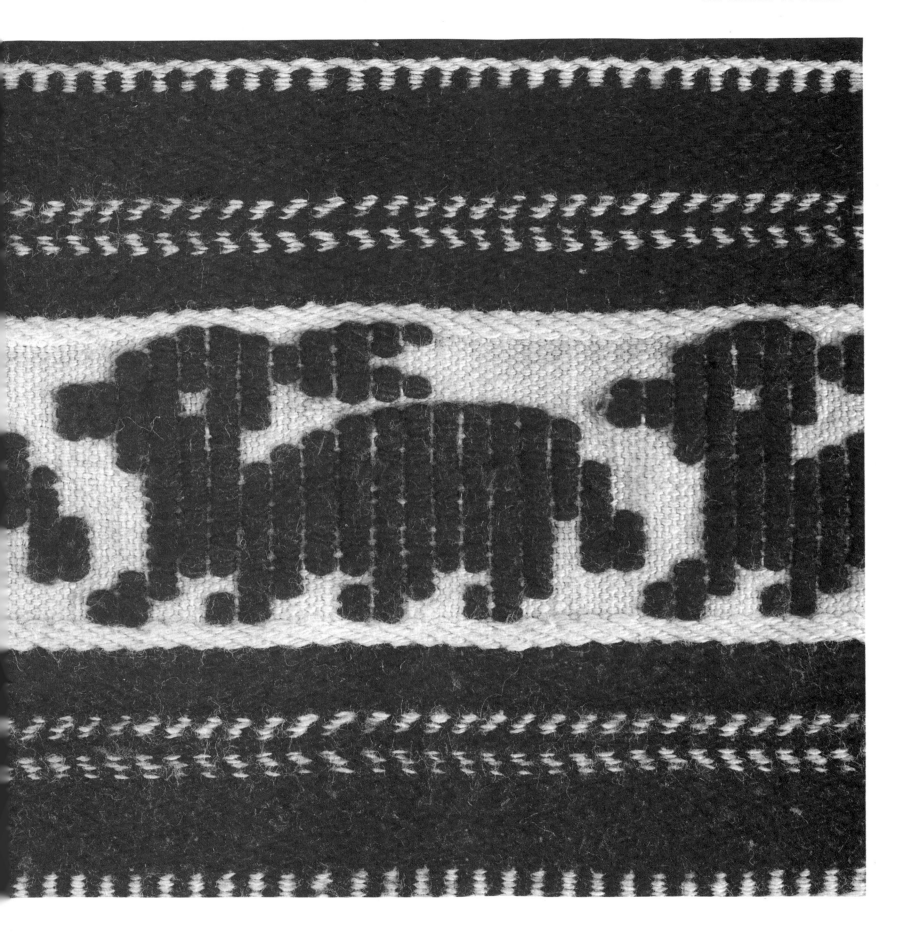

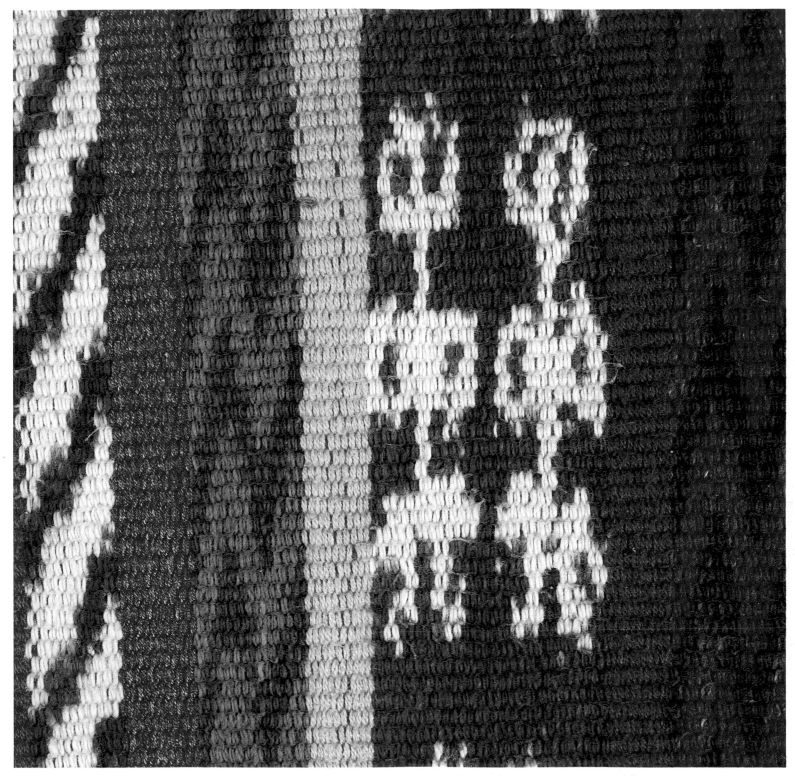

(*left*) Shawl, Santo Domingo Xenacoj, Sacatepequez district; Cakchiquel tribe.

Shawl, Totonicapán, Totonicapán district; Quiché tribe. A combination of geometric forms arranged in chevrons with *muñecas*, or little dolls.

Chichicastenango: religious brotherhood. Along with the municipal organization of local mayors, there is also a traditional organization of *principales*, whose function is to look after religious and civil life in the community. They are prepared for their future role from a very early age and before taking on the responsibility must rise through the successive levels of a local career.

Market at Chichicastenango. In the past it was easy to recognize which village someone came from by the colour and design of their clothes. Now, these differences are being lost; textiles are becoming less and less characteristic of a given region, and almost all *huipiles* are now machine-sewn and decorated with big, gaudy flowers. Each village continues to have its market day, which is still colourful, but less and less authentic.

On the road to the market in the Quezaltenango region.

Elaborate head-dress, seen at the Sacapulas market.

Quezaltenango, 2335m above sea level and approximately 200km from Guatemala City, is the second largest town in the country. It has always acted political and cultural capital of the zone of the *altos*, or high plains. The town stands in the middle of the Sierra Madre, dominated by the volcanoes which surround it – Zunil, Santa María and Santiagito. Cerro del Baul, featured here, is where the souls of the dead would endeavour to penetrate the other world; in the crevices the shamans secretly celebrate ritual ceremonies called *costumbres*.

Huipil, San Pedro Sacatepequez, San Marcos district; Mam tribe. Embroidery of flowers sewn onto the woven fabric.

Man's scarf, San Sebastian Huehuetenango,
Huehuetenango district; Mam tribe.

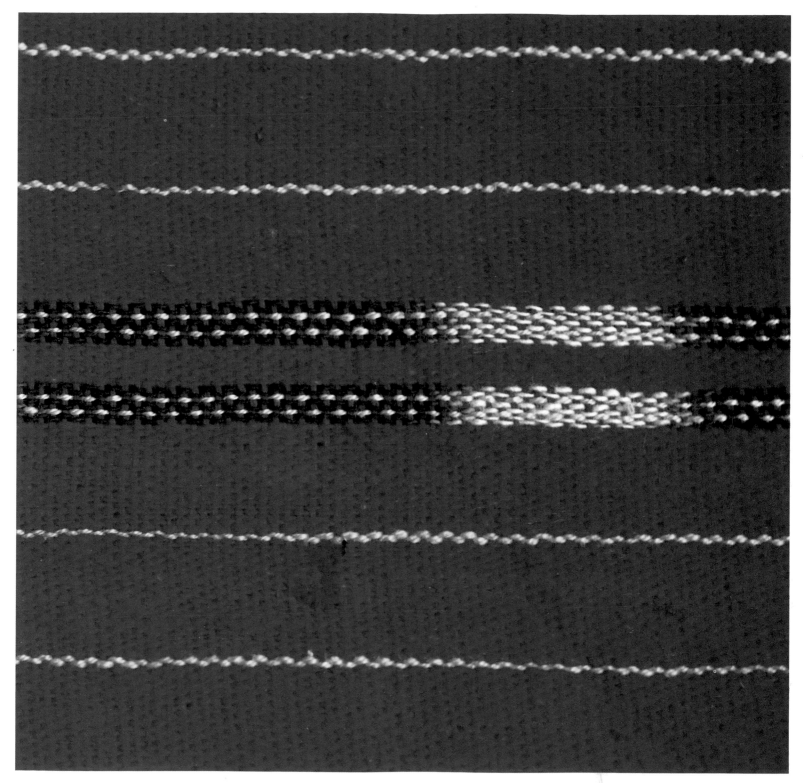

Skirt, San Sebastian Coatan, Huehuetenango district;
Mam tribe.

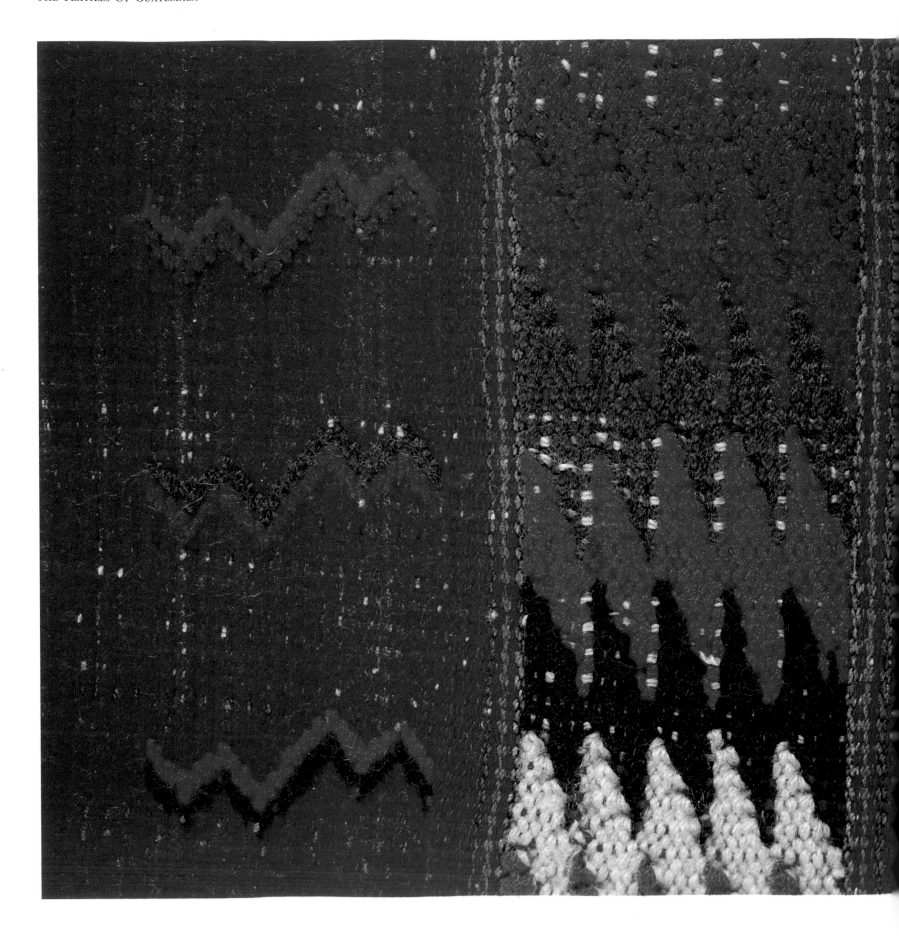

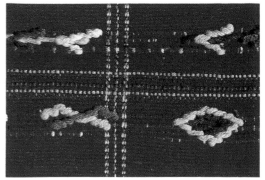

Man's tzut, San Sebastian
Huehuetenango, Huehuetenango
district; Mam tribe.

Huipil, Todos Santos Cuchumatanes,
Huehuetenango district; Mam tribe.
Geometric pattern of lozenges and a
series of chevrons representing lightning.

Man's belt, Nebaj district; Ixil tribe.

Huipil, Chajul, Quiché district; Ixil tribe. Two humming-birds, seen here in profile and representing good and evil, rather than male sexual power, the bird's usual symbolic association. The lozenges represent the world with its four cardinal points and its cubic centre with the sacred tree of the ancient Mayas.

Woman's scarf, Nebaj, Quiché district; Ixil tribe. The women dress their hair in a great variety of ways. This piece of fabric is wrapped around the hair, the ends falling in large pompoms to frame the face.

Woman's belt, San Martín Chile Verde, Quezaltenango district; Mam tribe. Mountain cat crouching and eating corn. Hidden in his sacred grotto, the cat allowed men to appropriate corn for their use. Shown here with humming-birds and protecting a tobacco plant, he is linked to the love of the Sun and the Moon.

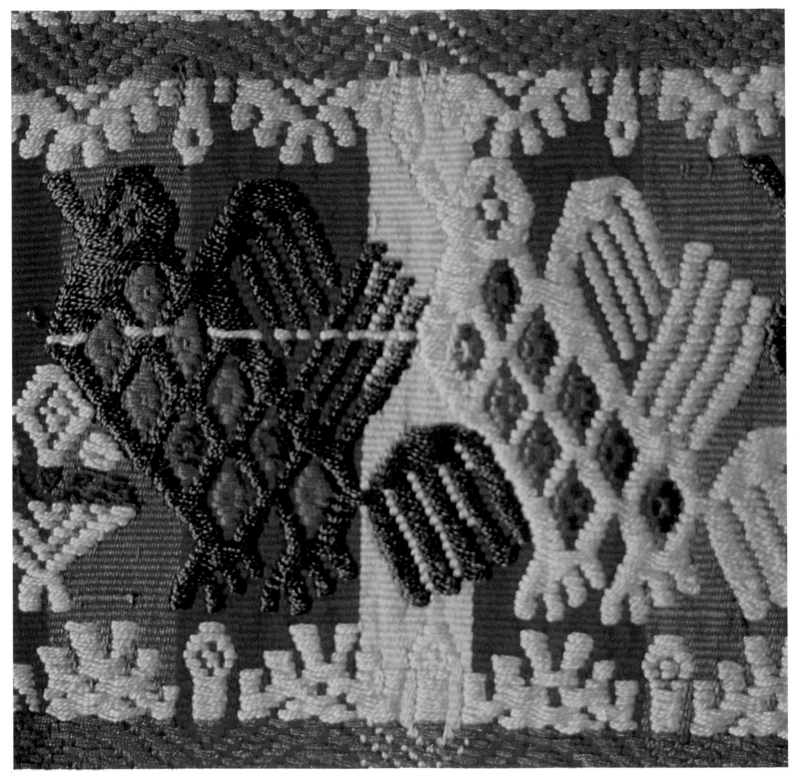

Woman's tzut, San Juan de Sacatepequez, Guatemala district; Cakchiquel tribe. The lozenge design is here used to symbolize the chicken, which was a popular and well-known bird even in Maya times.

El Baul, Pacific coast of Guatemala. On an ancient pyramid, still half-protected by the forest's cover, the local Indians carry out an ancient ceremony in an open-air shrine. In the shimmering candlelight, chickens, flowers, corn, beans and alcohol are offered in sacrifice to an ancient stone idol.

Petén, North Guatemala district. View of the Rio San Pedro. This is one of the main areas of Maya civilization (Tikal, Uaxactun), situated in the warm lower regions of the Petén forest. Today, the jungle which covered these ruins has been cleared away so that we can admire what remains of this great culture.

Huipil, Palo Gordo, San Marcos district; Mam tribe. Cockerel.

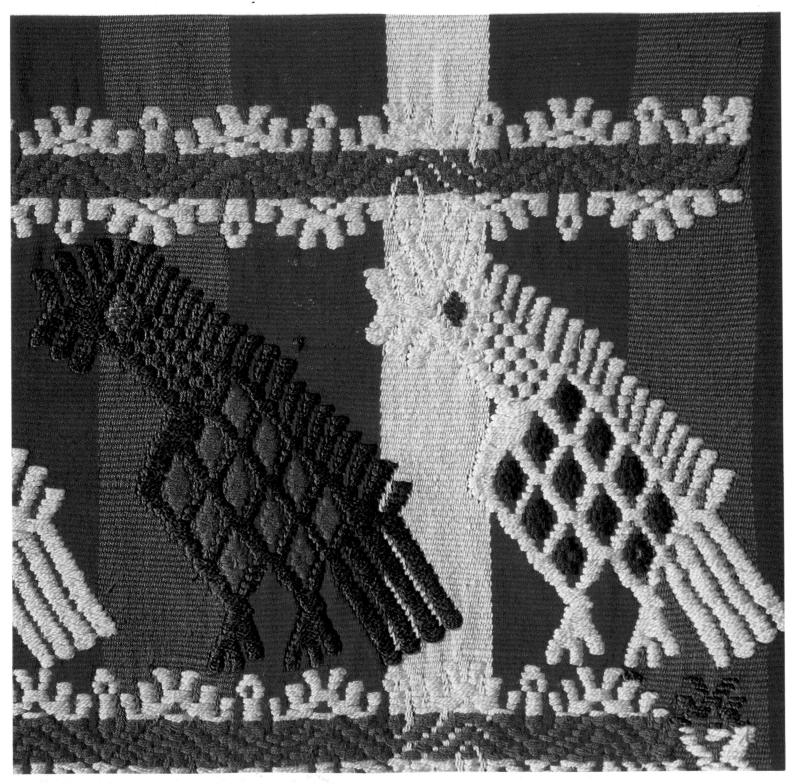

Woman's tzut, San Juan Sacatepéquez, Guatemala district;
Cakchiquel tribe. The mythical bird of the Cakchiquels,
the *muan*.

Huipil, Panajachel, Sololá district; Cakchiquel tribe. Cats.

A typical house on the high plains, with corn drying on the verandah.

Skirt, Comitancillo, Quiché district.

Man's tzut, Colotenango,
Huehuetenango district; Mam tribe.

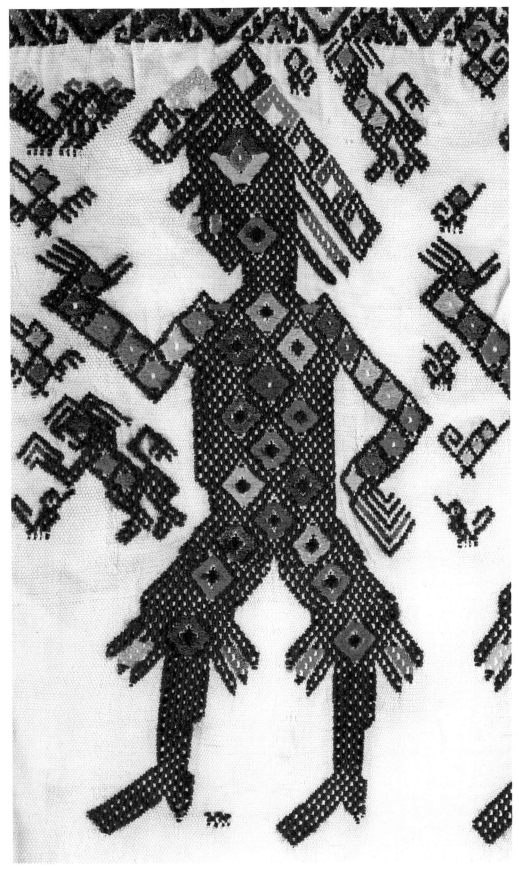

(*opposite*) Woman's tzut, Coban, Alta Verapaz district; Kekchi tribe. Gauze with bands of woven material alternating with brocade, decorated with little figures and stylized birds.

(*left*) Huipil, Nahualá, Sololá district; Quiché tribe. Stylized representation of half-man, half-jaguar.

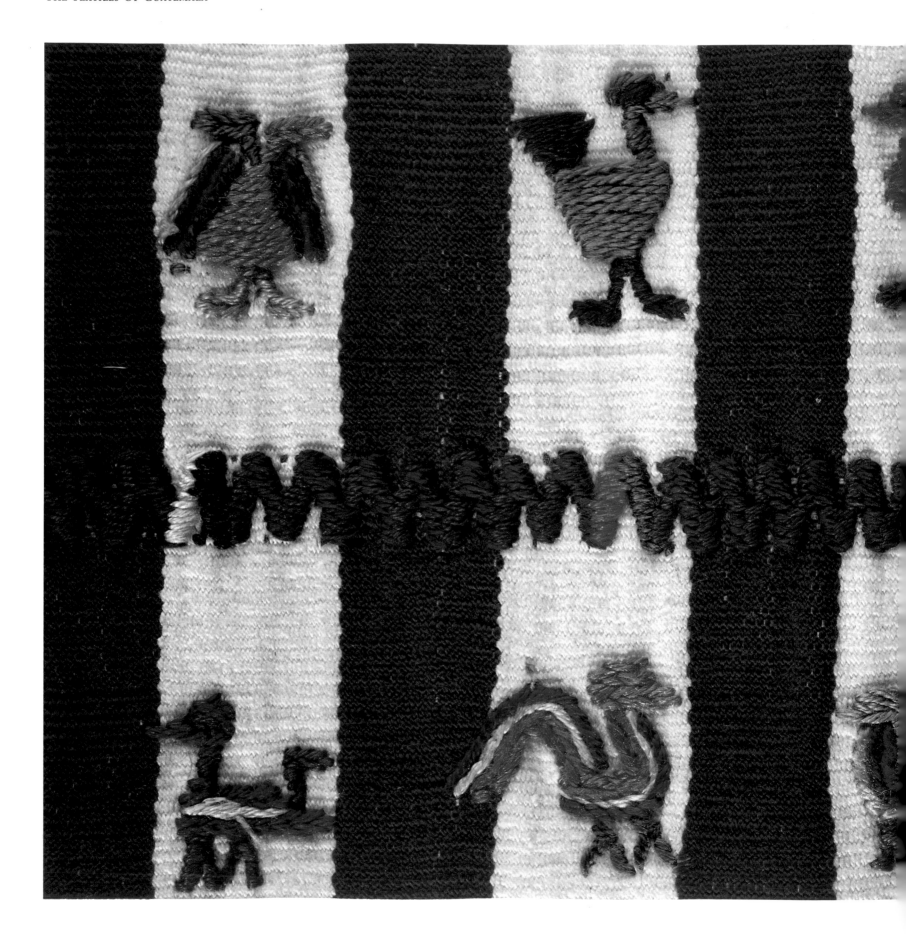

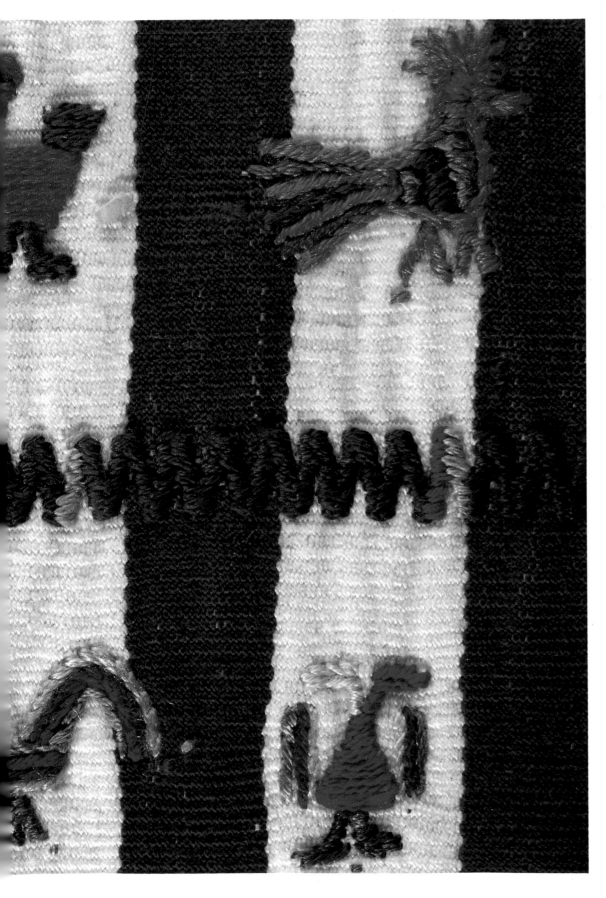

Lake Atitlán is a volcanic lake 1,500m above sea level, with a circumference of around 120km and spanning 18km at its widest point. Its name means 'ancestor of water'. The lake is surrounded by mountains and in the south three large volcanoes dominate its waters: Toliman (3280m), Atitlán (3505m), San Pedro (3025m) and a fourth, smaller one which is called San Lucas. A particularity of the lake is that its source has not yet been discovered; it is thought that there is an underground outlet.

Man's trousers, Santiago Atitlán, Sololá district; Tzutujil tribe. Representation of little birds, found on the borders of Lake Atitlán, where Santiago Atitlán is itself situated.

(*opposite*) Skirt, Piedras Grandes, San Marcos district; Mam tribe. This style of skirt is very close-fitting and reaches the ground, completely covering the feet. The close cut of the cloth gives the women a very graceful walk and a particular way of sitting. The cloth is generally made on foot looms. This example in yellow silk is characteristic of the Mam region south of San Marcos. The colour yellow is obtained from a root called *camotillo*.

(*left*) Huipil, San Miguel Ixchiguan, San Marcos district; Mam tribe. Dragons.

Huipil, Almolonga, Quezaltenango district; Quiché tribe. Characteristic geometric forms are placed on a diagonal axis on the *huipil*.

Huipil, Patzun, Chimaltenango district; Cakchiquel tribe.

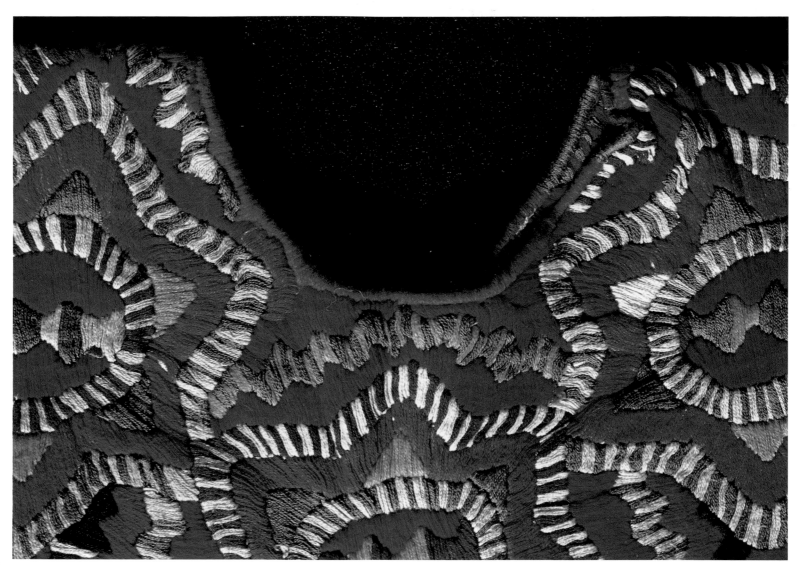

Huipil, San Mateo Ixtatan, Huehuetenango district; Chuj tribe.

(*above*) Huipil, Panajachel, Sololá district; Cakchiquel tribe. Symbolic representation of a duck. Ducks are to be found on the borders of Lake Atitlán, where Panajachel is situated.

(*below*) Huipil, Alotenango, Sacatepequez district; Cakchiquel tribe.

Huipil, Cakchiquel tribe (page 94), Chillani (Guatemala). Symbolic representation of the Jaguar, animal often associated with the symbol of sun during its journey into the underworld.

Barriletes, or kites at Santiago Sacatepequez. This looks like a simple competition to fly these enormous kites, but the origins of this event lie deep in the indigenous traditions of Guatemala. On the day of the dead, November 1, enormous circular constructions made of willow frames and decorated with multicoloured fabrics and painted oiled paper are flown over the cemetery at Santiago Sacatepequez. These kites are sometimes as big as six metres in diameter. This event, as well as being a competition of size and design, is also a way of communicating between the Indians of today and their dead ancestors.

Woman's shawl, Patzun, Chimaltenango district;
Cakchiquel tribe. Stylized representation of a floral motif.

Woman's scarf, San Juan Ostumaleo, Quezaltenango district; Mam tribe. Geometric forms representing the 'Yaxche', the Maya tree of life, which lies at the centre of Maya cosmology. The tree is supposed to greet men and women in the after-life, and is worshipped by burning incense; it is associated with the symbol of the snake.

Woman's belt, Colotenango, Huehuetenango district;
Mam tribe.

Woman's scarf, San Andres Sajcabaja, Quiché district; Quiché tribe.

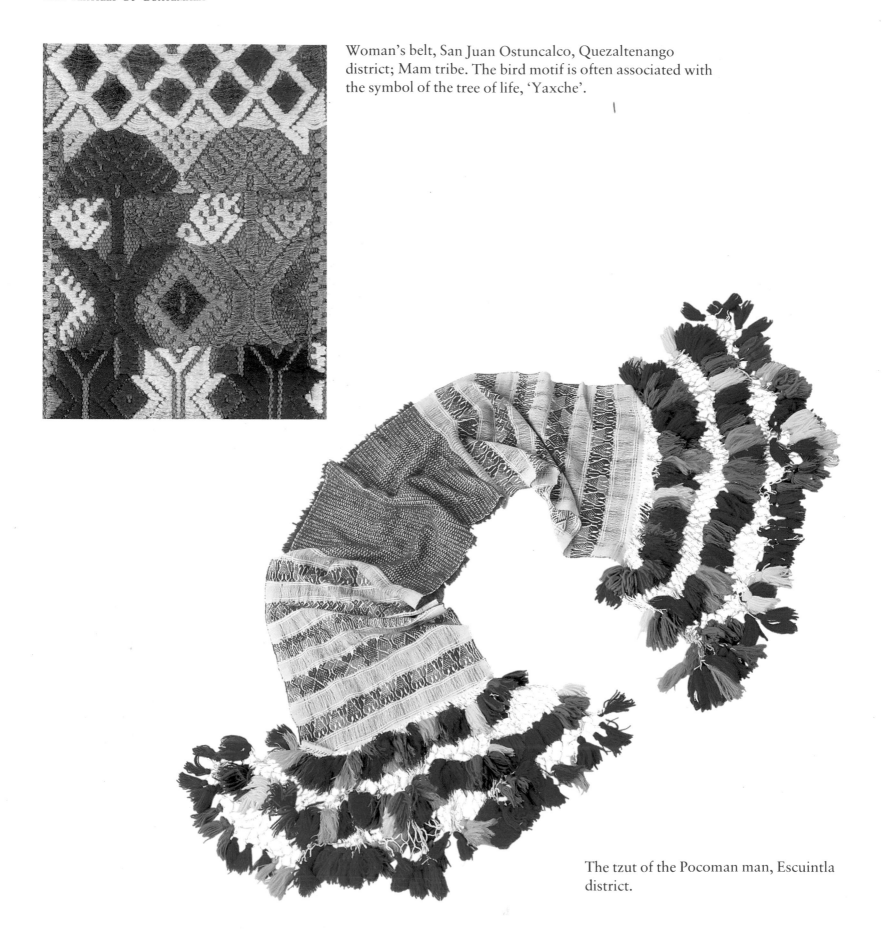

Woman's belt, San Juan Ostuncalco, Quezaltenango district; Mam tribe. The bird motif is often associated with the symbol of the tree of life, 'Yaxche'.

The tzut of the Pocoman man, Escuintla district.

Huipil, San Mateo Ixtatan chuj, Huehuetenango district.
Geometric decorative motifs, symbolising the four phases
of sun and moon. The sun is the centre of the Maya
cosmos.

Woman's belt, San Juan Sacatepequez, Guatemala district; Cakchiquel. The skirts of the woman are held up by belts. These are decorated in a wide variety of ways, the different colours and symbols distinguishing their villages. Those of San Juan are very wide and very highly decorated. The figure of the monkey is easy to recognize and features in many myths, still appearing in ritual dances today. The dance of the Micos or the Monos is a reminder of the episode in the *Popol Vuh*, the sacred book of the ancient Quiché Mayas, in which men are changed into monkeys.

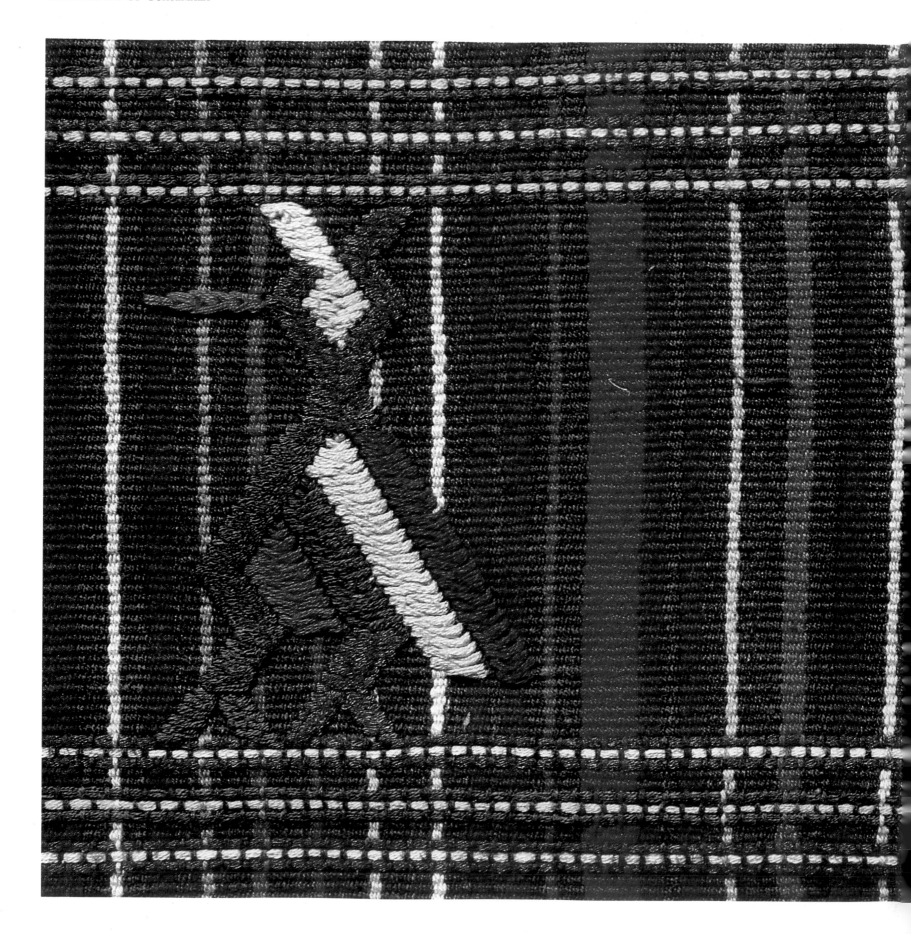

Woman's tzut, Chajul, Quiché district;
Ixil tribe.

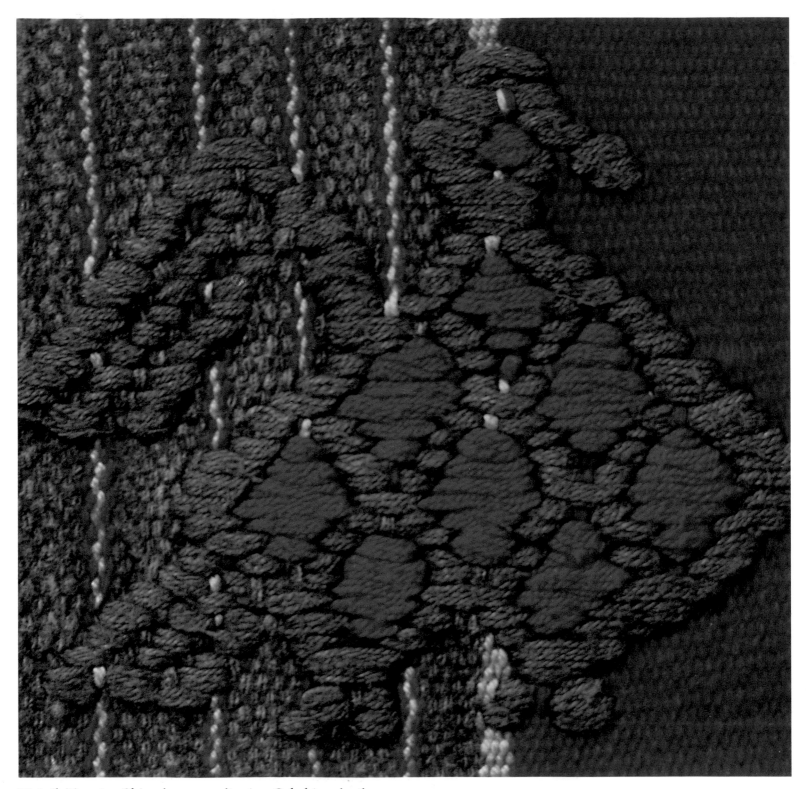

Huipil, Tecpán, Chimaltenango district; Cakchiquel tribe.
Bird. The colour brown comes from *ixcacao* fibre or
cuyuscate of cotton. It can also be obtained from alder
bark.

Huipil, San Juan Sacatepequez, Guatemala district;
Cakchiquel tribe. Peacock.

Huipil, Tecpán, Chimaltenango district; Cakchiquel tribe.
Bird represented with lozenges, thus associated with the
creation of the world.

Man's belt, San Martin Chile Verde, Quezaltenango district; Mam tribe. Symbolic representation of a peacock and a sacred *ceiba*, or alder tree.